The Sonnets

of a

Handsome and Well-Mannered

Rogue

of a Handsome

TRANSLATED FROM

CECCO   ANGIOLIERI

OF SIENA

Thomas Caldecot Chubb

The Sonnets

and Well-Mannered

Rogue

Archon Books

1970

ISBN: 0 208 010343
Library of Congress Catalog Card Number: 73-114193
PRINTED IN THE UNITED STATES OF AMERICA

To
Herman W. Liebert

Good friend of books and
of those who write
them

INTRODUCTION

The Sonnets of a Handsome & Well Mannered Rogue

On a momentous morning — and knowing the Florentine spring and early summer, we dare hope it was both balmy and jocund — either late in May or during the first week of June in the year 1265, there was understandable rejoicing in one of the small brown houses that fronted the little church and tower of San Martino del Vescovo (even then old, they were begun in 986) not far from the Badia from whose bells citizens "still heard terce and none" tolled with bronze reverberation through the clear air.

The reason: a child, their first, had been born during the night to that sharp trader and self-proclaimed aristocrat Alighiero II di Bellincione degli Alighieri and his wife Gabriella (she was called Bella) di Durante di Scolaio degli Abbati who was really noble. And not merely a first child, but a son.

There was rejoicing again almost a year later — "sometime just after the third Sunday in Lent" — when this same dark-eyed infant was carried to the ancient Baptistery which faced the later torn-down cathedral of Santa Reparata, some of whose foundations, it is thought, were those uncovered underneath the present day Duomo by the 1966 flood. There he would be one of the five or six thousand who were simultaneously made Christians in the mass baptism which took place just once each year.

Rejoicing, and some celebration. It was customary in those days to give a private feast with much drinking of the heady Tuscan wine and eating of the already famous Florentine food in honor of each newly baptised babe, and this surely Alighiero and Bella did. These were occasions for much talk, and also, congratulations. As, therefore, godfather and godmother, as uncles and aunts, as cousins and even a few selected neighbors, poked and prodded the little boy who was just about to become a toddler, they made sure that Alighiero and Bella — but particularly Alighiero — would realize their good fortune.

"Durante di Alighiero degli Alighieri!" (Today we call him Dante Alighieri.) "Named after Bella's father, too. That was a prudent choice. It will please the Abbati and it is useful to please them. But most of all, not a daughter, but a son."

A son, the implication was, who would follow in the footsteps of his father who was now in his fifties and ready to be followed. A son who would in due course gradually take over the penny-grubbing business of this sharp and shrewd descendant of the knight crusader, Cacciaguida, and of the loftily-born Roman Frangipani who, under Charlemagne's orders, had helped rebuild the city after it had been destroyed "by Attila, the cruel Vandal". A son who would be as willing as Alighiero had been to add not so much florin to florin as *soldo* to *soldo* in money-lending that was close to usury and in land speculations of which the best that could be said was that "they were engaged in a *more* or *less* above board manner, *more* or *less* honestly."

Not one of those present, however — I think this is safe to say — was prescient enough to congratulate Alighiero and his wife for begetting a son who would become what Dante became.

Not one of them could or would divine that less than a century later, the second greatest of early Italian writers, Giovanni Boccaccio, would refer to this son as "the glory of the Italian race".

Obviously, no one could divine either, that six hundred years after Dante's birth, an eminent scholar living in a then undiscovered land, parts of which, it turned out, were not too distant from Dante's imaginary mountain of Purgatory, that this scholar would be able to say this of his masterwork:

"The *Commedia* may fairly claim to be the greatest single poem in our tradition. T.S. Eliot says that after Shakespeare and Dante, 'there is no third', but there is no single work of Shakespeare that can be compared to it in its scope."

Thomas Caldecot Chubb

Professor Bergin's is a statement hard not to accept. Indeed, in my judgement, the only single western poem that can even enter the lists against it is Homer's *Odyssey* (not his *Iliad*) but although the *Odyssey* perhaps equals the *Commedia* in artistry, when you match its geography against Dante's cosmography, it is not hard to see which is the more stupendous.

The story behind the Florentine's mighty creation is well-known. Near, if not next door to the Alighieri lived a very pretty girl — she was the daughter of a wealthy, prominent and public-spirited financier, Folco Portinari — and her name was Beatrice, or Bice, Portinari. Dante met her at a May Day festival, and thereafter, as young men will, he often looked at her with pulses quickening, while she, as young ladies will, alternately smiled at him and turned up her nose. Alighiero's son also wrote some sonnets to her. Not all of them were great or even good.

Then when she was twenty-three and already married to a young banker, Simone de' Bardi (Dante was twenty-five) she died, and in due course, and after more than one more than sideways glance at other young ladies, he collected these sonnets and certain others he had written to or about her into a small book. He added some explanation in prose which was in part literal and in part allegorical, and called this, his first published work, the *Vita Nuova*. But even that was not enough. He had to do more for Beatrice and said so.

"After this sonnet" — the last sonnet in the *Vita Nuova* — "there appeared to me a wondrous dream which made me decide to write nothing more about this blessed one until such time as I could treat of her more worthily. So that if it be the pleasure of Him by which all things live that my life continue for some few more years, I hope to write of her what has been written of no other women."

His life did so continue — for three more decades, to be precise — and he so wrote of her. When just before he died in 1321, he had penned the *Commedia's* triumphant last line, the little girl whom he had first met when he was nine, she seven, had become (according to the commentator you read) either Beatitude, or Theology, or the Ideal Church, or the Ideal Woman, and in one of these capacities she had gone down from Heaven to Hell to bid Virgil to guide Dante toward heaven; she had met the poet — and sharply questioned him — at the threshhold of the Earthly Paradise; and she had finally led Him to the very presence of God himself (who took the form of an inordinately intense concentrated point of light) and to the love that moves the sun and the other stars.

He had fulfilled his pledge, for certainly no other woman had been written about in this way. Petrarch's Laura — a pale descendant of Beatrice — to the contrary notwithstanding, no women would ever be written about in this way again.

No other poem, either, had been so original.

But original as the poem was — even the meter, *terza rima* was invented by Dante, supposedly to further canonize the number three, which (with nine and ten) had a symbolic meaning to him — certain of its moods and even its techniques had predecessors.

Woman worship, particularly woman worship by a poet, was one of them. This began in Provence — according to an American novelist of this century, it was there called *domnei* — where it inspired a whole school of poetry. It then — modified, of course, as it naturally would have been with this change of locale — moved to the court of Frederick II in Sicily where it produced "the Notary", Jacopo Lentini, and others. Next it went to Tuscany and Emilia (Fra Guittone of Arezzo and Guido Guincelli of Bologna), and finally it localized itself in Florence. Dante called it the *dolce stil novo*. Whether he invented this term or merely set down one in general critical use, it was a good one.

The *Commedia*, however, did not derive only from this Southern France poetry of woman worship gradually transmuted into the sweet new style. Certain of its techniques were based on something somewhat more earthly. Side by side with the notes played on the dulcet harps of love was another kind of poetry whose nature is well described in the title of A.F. Massèra's anthology: *Sonetti burleschi e realistici dei primi due secoli.* Burlesque and realistic! In the critical concern with Dante's high moral purpose and lofty vision, is more often than not forgotten that even in his *Commedia,* his poetry more than occasionally fitted into one of these categories.

Particularly into the realistic category, and this especially in the *Inferno* and the *Purgatorio.* In these two realms of the unforgiven and those who are painfully winning their way to forgiveness, his portraiture is often that of a candid camera, the conversations he sets down seem to have been tape recorded. But he did use the burlesque too — and not merely in his *tenzone* with Forese Donati which finds a place in the Massèra collection. For an example, turn to cantos XXI and XXII of the *Inferno* (the hell of the barratrors — and remember Dante himself was accused of barratry) where the demons Rubicante, Graffiacane, Cagnazzo and others (their names all parodies of the names of notable Florentine families) amuse themselves by throwing struggling sinners into a lake of boiling pitch.

For that reason, and because of the biting and incisive merit of most of these burlesque and realistic poems, and because there were many, many more of them than poems in the style of Dante's early poems to Beatrice, and those of Guido Cavalcante (Dante's "first friend"), and Cino da Pistoia, they are worth considering — especially by English-speaking readers who have largely neglected them.

Their subjects were as various in their nature as they could possibly be, for in those days, as I have pointed out elsewhere, you wrote a poem where today you would write a letter to the editor; or a book review; or an epistle offering thanks, condolences or congratulations; or anything else that came into your mind. You wrote a poem, for example, on how to be a businessman or to become a knight. The Compiuta Donzella (the accomplished damsel) wrote on her own subjects from a young lady's point of view.

But even the same author often ventured into different and not related fields. Take Rustico Filippi, the dedicated — and talented — Ghibelline, fifty eight of whose sonnets appear in the Massèra volume. He could gibe at the Guelphs "who quaking ran away" after Montaperto only to come back to Florence, heads high, when Charles of Anjou had won their war for them at Benevento; move on to attack a staid citizen for seemingly being more interested in a pretty boy than in his lady love; poke fun at a girl who allowed herself to grow too thin; heap scorn on Lambertuccio Frescobaldo for his alleged avarice; cariacature one Messer Messerin whose neck was "like a duck's long, tough, and thin"; and end up with a series of love poems addressed to a lady who he hoped would greet him not in heaven but on this sinful earth. I select at random. Rustico deals with many another subject in that part of his work preserved by Massèra. Other of the "realistic and burlesque" writers strayed similarly into similarly diverse fields.

Nor was their concept of realism always, or even often, the same. Some of them — Folgore da San Gimignano, for example — wove a rich and brocaded tapestry. Others, like Cenne della Chitarra, turned to the sordid and the drab.

Each of these two, for example, wrote a sonnet sequence on the months of the year, but oh how different they were! Folgore begins thus:

> I give you for the month of January
> Courtyards and halls where fires flame and flair;
> Beds and bedchambers furnished handsomely
> With silken sheets and coverlets of vair.

He then continues to describe throwing snowballs at "the fair damosels who stand around" in that same first month of the year; the hunt in February; fishing in March; the flowers and green grass of April; jousting in May; riding from castle to castle in June; and so on through the year.

Guitar-playing Cenne describes another kind of Italy:

> For January I do give to ye
> A smoke-filled mountain hold — full drear they are —
> With beds like bunks on ship from Genoa,
> And rainy winds that never warm will be.
> Of lack of girls I give a plethora;
> For drink, Calabrian vinegar, sour, strong;
> For clothes, the kind of stuff that leaves half bare
> Some lean varlet whose place has vanished long.

After that he takes you to "an ice-gripped vale where huge bears are" and where you can "a-hunting go in boots that leak" (February); to "Apulia's flat, miasmal lagoon" (March); to the Romagna where you joined "a mule train" whose mule "that brayed" made it very hard to evade the Romagna customs officers in search of smuggled goods (April); and thus, always unpleasantly, from June to December which was the dreariest month of all.

Cenne makes it this, for, says he, in December;

> I will dump you in a fen
> With mud and ice, and you most scantily clad,
> Your food dried beans and pulse — both of them bad—
> Your host a Maremma rogue in his thieves' den,
> Your cook, scrawny and ugly, the worst of men.

Folgore, in contrast, in his December, offered, among other things, "roasted porker, cooked most temptingly;" wine out of "kegs as big as Galgan's monastery;" and for clothing:

> fur-lined cloak
> And fur-lined robe, and fur-trimmed tabard, vest,
> And capes, fashionably made, with well-stitched hem.

These, then, and men like them, were the *poeti realistici e burleschi* who so fascinated Massèra and others, and of them none was more prolific and more important than Cecco Angiolieri of Siena, of whose writings I offer a translation in this book. Most prolific, because no other of these realistic and burlesque writers has left anything like Cecco's 150 sonnets behind him. Most important, because, on the whole, his is the best and the most vivid writing of this interesting school, and also because he was both the friend and the enemy of Dante on whom he exerted at least a little influence.

Like so many minor and even major figures who lived in the last days of the Italian Middle Ages, we have only a few really hard facts about his life. To be sure, Boccaccio deals with him in a lively manner, making him "the fall guy" whom another Cecco — Cecco Fortarrigo — diddles in *Decamerone* IX,4, but also describing him as "both a handsome man and a well-mannered one", in contrast to Fortarrigo who "was a gambler and at times a drunkard". It is possible that Giovanni had his two Ceccos mixed. At any rate, his description of Cecco Fortarrigo would also fit our Cecco.

Other than this, we know only the following:

1. That our poet was born in 1260 or very shortly before this, his father being one Angioliero degli Angelioleri who was twice one of Siena's priors and held other high offices in the commune, and his mother Lisa Salimbeni of the rich and ruling Salimbeni clan.

2. That in 1281 he served in the campaign against the little town of Turri in the Maremma, and in the same year was fined two *libbre* (pounds) for being AWOL.

3. That in 1282 he was fined thrice — twice for unauthorized military absences again, and once for caterwauling in the streets after the commune's bell had signified the curfew by sounding sonorously for the third time.

4. That in 1288, he and his father were paid for serving in the Sienese cavalry when it rode into the Casentino to help Florence in its war against Arezzo. This was the campaign which culminated in the battle of Campaldino in which Dante fought. Dante was also in the cavalry — the Florentine cavalry, of course — and it is thought that he and Cecco may have met then. Certainly they knew each other, and may have known each other well. More than one of Cecco's sonnets clearly indicate this,

Thomas Caldecot Chubb

especially if one concludes that Sonnet 137 is Cecco's contribution to a lost *tenzone* comparable to Dante's *tenzone* with Forese Donati.

5. That in 1291 Cecco was again fined for not observing the curfew, and in the same year he was formally accused of stabbing Dino di Bernardino of Monteluco. However, the charges appear to have been dropped.

6. That at about this time — at any rate some time between 1291 and 1302 — he was banished from Siena, and according to one authority "went to Rome where he was given shelter in the house of Cardinal Riccardo Petroni of Siena." Boccaccio (again in *Decamerone* IX,4) tells the story differently. Cecco was not banished, but "it seeming to him that he could live but badly in Siena on the allowance given him by his father, and hearing that a certain cardinal (Cardinal Petroni), a great patron of his, had come to the Marches of Ancona as papal legate, decided to go there in the hope of bettering his condition." He persuaded his father to give him six months' allowance in advance, and off he went.

7. That in 1302, he sold a vineyard to Neri Perini for 700 *Libbre*. Despite his complaints about his poverty which we will find in his poetry, he could not have been a pauper.

8. That he had died before 1313 (in all probability he had died in 1312) in which year his sons Meo, Deo, Angioliero and Simone, and his daughter, Arbolina, renounced all claims to his estate on the grounds that it was worthless on account of their father's debts. See sonnets 89 and 91 for references to their mother, Cecco's wife who may be the "other pear" of Sonnet 51.

These things are documented, and are not subject to contradiction, but they are not all we know, or think we know, about Cecco. We know, for example — and can feel reasonably certain that we really know, for he was not oversupplied with reticence and "tells all" in his poetry — that he violently hated his father whom he regarded as both rich, close-fisted and hypocritical, and whose ostentatious supposed piety (Angioliero was a lay brother of the *frate gaudente*) could not have been more revolting to him. We know (also from his sonnets) that he hated his mother too, and for the same reasons. (He hated her even more when after his father's death, one Mino Zeppa — Mino the troublemaker, who, or so Cecco was convinced — had persuaded her to hold back his inheritance from him.) We know that he was long and wordily in love with a girl of the Sienese lover classes, Becchina (in English she would be Becky for Rebecca), the daughter of a genial leather worker named Benci. Except for one glorious occasion — it was on July 20, 1291 as he notes in Sonnet 38 — she remained cold or even hostile in the face of his advances until she was married. Then she complained because he did not protect her from her husband. Finally, we know that after his pursuit of Becchina came to end, he at least skirted the edges of a homosexual involvement. But that was not uncommon in those days.

Out of this kind of life, out of these experiences and others — Sonnets 47 and 96 confirm that he was indeed an exile, and Sonnet 137 that at least part of this exile was spent in Rome; Sonnet 141 that he had either been to Germany or had a friend who had been there; Sonnets 142 and 143 that he had lived in the gutter for a while or close enough to it to learn its jargon; and Sonnet 99 that Boccaccio (as we have already suggested) was wrong and that he was the Cecco who loves "women and throwing dice and drinking wine" — out of all this, his amazing collection of poetry was born.

The sonnets to and about Becchina form its greatest part. In fact not until Sonnet 73 do we find a poem that does not deal with her, and he still finds it appropriate to refer to her as near the end of his collection as Sonnet 135. They are love sonnets of a very offbeat kind. Dante might have understood them — note I say *might* not *would* — but Petrarch would

Thomas Caldecot Chubb

have wrapped himself in his cloak of prissiness and shuddered.

They strike every note and celebrate every possible mood. In Sonnet 1, Cecco cries "Stop thief! Stop thief! I have been robbed!" — of his heart, of course! — and Becchina replies to the effect that she is delighted. Then in Sonnet 2, he does a spin, and tells his low-born lady love (see Sonnet 72 in which he describes her make-up) that because he has become her slave, she is of nobler lineage than he is. Another sonnet (Sonnet 6) is such a litany of "alas's" intricately interwoven that one wonders if Cecco were not more interested in his writing ingenuity than in his lady. (Other sonnets, too many to name, take us in the same direction.) A fourth sonnet (Sonnet 12) wishes that Becchina would hate him and not merely be indifferent while a fifth reverses the field to say that she wishes he would die. He will not, however, he says, for that would too greatly please her father (the genial leather tanner!) who evidently had some reservations about this scion of the upper classes playing around with his daughter. A sixth — but it would use up more space than would be useful to go through the whole long list.

Then gradually (beginning with Sonnets 60 and 61) a new theme is introduced. The light of his eyes, he discovers, is a dedicated gold-digger. The reason she pushes aside his attentions is "because florins do not bulge my purse", and the reason they do not, he also realizes, is the stinginess of his father. Then and there his famous hate begins — his hate (Sonnet 71) of his father, and shortly, of his mother. It reached its peak of fury in Sonnet 98 — "if I were fire I would burn up the world!" — which is the best-known and the most frequently quoted of anything he wrote. It was a violent manifestation of what today we call the generation gap, showing that there is little new under the sun. It burst forth in an incredible fourteen lines that are as red-hot and savage as the lava and cinders shot forth by Vesuvius or Etna.

Nor did this hatred end even when he had thus erupted. He hated his father until the latter died, at which time he changed his tune and wrote a smug sonnet (Sonnet 109), in which he stated that "he who says aught but good bout his sire should have his tongue sliced off with a sharp blade". We have no record that his hatred for his mother ever ended. It was perhaps more bitter than his hatred of his father. The worst that he ever said about his father was that he did not keep him sufficiently supplied with money. He accused his mother (Sonnets 113, 114 and 115) of trying to poison him.

Compared with the Becchina sonnets and those dealing with his parents, the rest of Cecco's writing is possibly less significant, but most of it is no less readable. I particularly commend Sonnet 137 (the Dante sonnet of the lost *tenzone*); Sonnet 137 (about how puffed up one Neri Picciolini was when he returned from France — as many still are today); Sonnet 138 (the Germany Sonnet); Sonnet 148 (a fable about the jackass who thought he was a stag); and Sonnet 149, which may be an attack upon plagiarism. I hope you will at least read these.

But in my heart, I hope you will read all 150. Most of them deserve this on their own merits. They will also help you to understand one aspect of the age in which Cecco lived, and, as I have suggested earlier, one of the contemporary points of view that had some influence on that age's greatest man and greatest writer.

T.C.C.
Greenwich, October 1969

1.

Accorri, accorri, accorri, uom, a la strada!

Cecco and a Passerby

"Stop thief! Stop thief! Stop thief! Help! Succor! Aid!
"What's wrong, you whoreson rogue!" "My treasure's been
    ta'en!"
"Who's taken it?" "A lady, I tell you plain,
Who shaves as does a razor keenly made!"
Then why do you not stab her with your blade?
"I'd rather stab myself!" *"You must be crazed!"*
"Perhaps. What makes you think so?" *"You walk as dazed
Or blinded — from your senses you have strayed!"*

Becchina and Cecco

"You see now what sane people think you are!"
"Dare you say that, who robbed me?" *"Get you gone!"*
"I do, but slowly, weeping piteously."
"And with what heart?" "Ah, woeful, woebegone!"
"Then on you light all curses that there are."
"Now you have slain me!" *"The devil — that's naught to me!"*

Avvenga ched i' paghi'l tu mirare

If I should, dear, repay you for a glance
With riches that befitted the world's lord,
What would you do for me in recompence?
Of your kind thoughts, could I be then assured?
Ah, but I pray you — let this be Love's gloze —
That you should have the wish to speak to me,
Nor scornfully and proud turn up your nose
Because, your slave, I am of less degree.
Why, even the noblest and the haughtiest
In duty must be humble, and courteous too.
Were this not so, then great would be the shame,
And you're not shamefull — but the sweetest and best
Of gracious ladies — this do I proclaim
Who now am yours and always will be true.

Or non è gran pistolenza la mia

Oh, am I not beset with the plague's pain
Since I cannot give over loving one
Who hates me — what is worse, has such disdain
She will not even glance as I pass on?
Yes, night and day she brings me such great woe
That agony with sweat my brow's besprent.
My soul burns, yet she does not care, I know.
I cannot think that Hell is different.
Often my friends saȳ: "Is she worth your grief?
She is a woman, that you realize,
And they are all the same, and that is ill."
Yet since I love her beyond all belief,
I wait for Love to aid in my emprise.
All potent, he can do so if he will.

Thomas Caldecot Chubb

4.

Maladetto e distrutto sia da Dio

May God's destruction, and His curses too,
Light on that moment when I came to love
A woman whom naught else to joy can move
Than bringing me to anguish and to woe.
Yes, she has tortured me so, through and through,
That I believe no man has suffered so.
Yet even that to her is not enow
Whose heart is like the heart of wicked Jew.
Her only pleasure is to do me ill,
Such ill, indeed, that it will break my heart.
In this she has unswerving constancy.
Oh, would I could absolve me from her sway,
Who from my dazed mind makes all else depart
So that the dead have joys not known to me.

5.

I' ho sì poco grazia 'n Becchina

With my Becchina, I have such small grace
That by God's faith — and He does not deceive —
In her heart I can never find a place.
My woe nor drugs nor doctor can relieve.
She is as cruel to me as a Saracen
Or as King Herod, who the innocents slew,
Yet, spite this, at her lovely feet I strew
My praises and adore her as a queen.
Here is the error that she leads me to:
To kiss the sainted ground whereon she stands
Is now the only heaven I desire.
Ah, would she but exclaim: "This is for you!"
And put an iris flower into my hands
I'd live, who now to bitter death aspire.

6.

Oimè d'Amor, che m'è duce sì reo

Alas for Love, to me a lord so ill!
Alas, for no whit worse could be my lot!
Alas, O God, why was this thing begot?
Alas, I love as no man other will!
Alas, this lady who my heart doth slay!
Alas, why can I mercy ask nowhere?
Alas, why can she be Jew false, my fair?
Alas, my plaints, why hears she not alway?
Alas, and for that cursed and fatal hour,
Alas, in which her beauty I did see!
Alas, for at that time began my woe!
Alas, that seems a rose, a fresh sweet flower,
Alas, her face. Whence came the villany,
Alas, in her that makes her treat me so?

7.

Egli è sì agra cosa 'l disamare

To cast out love so hard a thing it be,
If you have truly loved, that I declare
To make black skins seem white far easier were,
The skins of folk that live beyond the sea.
But since I now would no more think of you
Though to adore you one time was my vow,
And since with wrath I am burned through and through,
May God bring this to pass some way, somehow.
Yet let not Love call this his diadem
That I would rather turn from love away,
If that I could, than be the Emperor.
I of his servants have been servitor
As long as I have lived — and, night and day
And had but woe. God give the same to him.

Thomas Caldecot Chubb

Quanto un granel di panico è minore

As much as seed of panic grass is less
Than lofty peak — he who has eyes, must know't;
As much as golden florin with its brightness
Is more than a cheap copper penny or groat;
As much as today's anguishes that grieve
Are more — I have them — than woes I used to have,
So much the greater are the pains of love
Than I had dreamed, or that I could believe.
Yet I believe it now, since now their fell
Sorrow has touched my soul so much that I
Would of this love and loving be quite clean.
Yet I can no more break its empery
Than chick, into this world from its egg shell,
Can come before its appointed hour has been.

9.

Io potrei cosi stare senz'amore

My love of love foreswear I can no more
Than Moco can give up his sodomy,
Or than good Ciampolin, that high liver,
Can live and not throw dice incessantly;
Nor more than Min di Pepo can forbear
From smiting Tano hard — his better he —
Nor Migo — who will not say Christian prayer —
Not die in flames for this, his heresy.
Therefore let Love do to me what he please,
Yet I his faithful servant will be still,
And with good heart accept the grief and pain.
What though it be as bitter as wine's lees?
My humble spirit — that shapes good out of ill —
Will make it sweet to me as sugarcane.

Quando veggio Becchina corrucciata

When I see my Becchina wroth at me,
Valiant though I am, who have a lion's heart,
I shake as does a schoolboy fearfully
Whose master canes his hand and makes it smart.
My soul cries: "Would that I had not been born
Rather than suffer now this misery!"
Cursed be the hour and season that brought to me
The anguish and the sorrow of her scorn.
Yet somehow — though my soul the devil gain
Because I say this — I must find a way
To cry: "A fig for her. Nay, let her rave!"
If not, then may death take me. This I say,
Nor do conceal it, but I make it plain:
I must, I will then, prove that I am brave!

11.

Io averò quell' ora un sol di bene

I have as bright a ray of joy today
As there is snow at Rome in high August,
But grief, sorrow, and pain — alackaday! —
Plentiful as October's wine and must.
And this — this evil thing — does only come
Because she has not a kind word for me,
But makes my heart beat full as woefully
As his who in deep Hell does have his home.
It is a sin she hates me so — a crime!
Why cannot her fierce war turn into peace?
I long to serve her — I do long to sore.
So I am as filled up with bitterness
As sea water boiled makes white and salty rime.
Yet she is wroth I do not suffer more.

La mia malinconia è tanta e tale

Such is my melancholy and so great
I cannot disbelieve a mortal foe
Would other do, if he my case should know
Than with a flood of tears commiserate.
For she, the cause of all, recks not my fate,
Or recks but little, though if she were lief,
She could, and straightway, cure me of my grief,
By saying to me only: "You I hate!"
Alas, I have from her but this refrain:
"I wish you neither hurt nor happiness;
Go you your way — let me go my way, sir!"
She cares not if I have or joy or pain.
Than straw beneath her feet she holds me less.
A curse on Love who gave me unto her!

13.

Èm m'è sì malamenta rincresciuto

This loving someone and not being loved
Filled me so evilly with such annoy
I turned my heart to stone and love removed.
Would I had done so sooner — that were joy!
For if I only earlier had grown wise,
It would have cost me far, far, far less pain.
My heart would now be whole, unbreathed my sighs,
And my hurt pride unwounded would remain.
Therefore, I say I do indeed do right
To love no more her who does not love me.
'T is plain as pikestaff. That I firmly state.
He who thinks differently to his own despite,
And will not change but holds fast steadfastly,
God grant he does not see the light too late.

14.

L'animo riposato aver solìa

Time was I always had a soul serene,
Nor did I even know that Sorrow was.
But now that Love holds me in his demesne,
I scarce believe there is aught else, alas.
Woe's me, how great have my misfortunes been
Since I became the slave of this cruel lord.
Whatever I do makes me seem worse, I ween,
To her who has for me nor thought nor word.
'T is indeed true not more than once or twice
Have I obeyed her who, did she but deign,
Could command me with her lifted finger even,
Yet I would leap from a high precipice
If, that I served her, I could thus make plain,
And should I die so doing, I'd be in heaven.

15.

Ciò, che fu naturalmente creato

All beings that by nature are create,
Whether of land or sea or of the air,
Acknowledge man as lord, must be obeyer
Of his commands, or else be held ingrate.
But so unnatured have I been by fate
That nothing of this do I know or feel
Once master, I'm now slave, crushed under heel,
Nor will I ever change this sorry state.
For I have been cast into the abyss —
I offer no excuse, none having found —
By following love that flits like butterfly.
My heart has done me great offense in this.
It has pinioned my shoulders hard against the ground,
Yet I must go this road eternally.

16.

Il cuore in corpo mi sento tremare

I feel within me my heart tremble so
Because of the great terror and great fear
I have, seeing and knowing my lady near,
I, who do fear to cause her the least woe;
Nor can I utter word, rash or discreet,
So does the strength that nature gave me fail.
Indeed, almost as miracle I hail
That I can even stand upon my feet.
Therefore, on those who pause as they pass by,
And see me wandering thus, and in a daze,
And cry: "Look at the wretch! He's in a swound!"
I do not heap abuse and blasphemy.
They're right. It is the truth that each one says.
Each day, each hour, I'm cast upon the ground.

17.

Chi vòl vantaggio aver a l'altre genti

He who would lord it over other folk,
Let him give loyally his heart to love,
Nor may he be called a friend who doth reprove
One who does this, nor name of cousin invoke.
Yea, may God make them woeful and heart-broke
Who speak of lovers other than in honor
Till they are like some hag with age upon her
Whose gums have lost all teeth in one fell stroke.
At that, he who serves my lady has lean fare.
That's my opinion. Of it I'm so sure
I'd gladly wager on it — this I say —
And if I lose, let ruin be my share.
I will not argue, but such woes endure
As Florence at Monte Aperto, that black day.

The Sonnets of A Handsome & Well Mannered Rogue   9

18.

Amor, poi ch'n sì greve passo venni

O Love, since I with steps so woebegone
Do walk, that all who see me cry: "Fie! Fie!"
And then of me so cruelly make fun
I have not words to tell it — no, not I —
Who of my five wits have been so undone,
And all my senses have gone so awry
That anyone must needs weep lamentably
If he saw worse. Then how shall I go on?
Yea, how not perish? Yet if the sweet aid
You give unto me ever should grow less,
My whole body would cry: "With fear I shake!"
Then though there's no reward or no crown made
That I can give to you, oh press, oh press
Your bit on me, nor ever it from me take.

19.

L'Amore, che m'è guerrèro ed enemico

Love, who has always been my enemy,
Has dealt with me as Michael with our Foe.
Now lit straws serve me for a candle's glow.
Judge, reader, how abject my misery!
Though but a youth, once old in wisdom I,
And have been called a fountain of good sense,
But, sure as Christ in heaven has residence,
That I have now gone mad, I don't deny.
Yet he who says that for this I'm to blame;
Sees through a broken mirror, does not see clear,
Since I against my will my wits have lost.
Is there no hope then in my grief and shame?
I see none. Only death at least and most.
So chatter as you will. I do not care.

Thomas Caldecot Chubb

20.

Quand i' solev'udir ch'un fiorentino

Of old, when I learned how this Florentine
Or that, had, through his grief, grown desperate,
And hanged himself, it seemed to me divine
Grace had abandoned him, so hard his fate.
But now I think it no more out of the way
Or strange for him to do than it would be
For one who had sawed marble all the day
To gulp a glass of wine down thirstily.
For now such sorrow I myself have known,
And agony and woe and grief and pain
That death would be a hundred thousand times less.
If you would learn how great my anguish has grown,
Read but my sonnets. There you will see plain
What I need scarcely two words to express.

21.

Se sì potesse morir di dolore

If it be true that man can die of woe,
Many are living now who should be dead,
And I am one, unless it can be said
I dwell already in the realms below.
Yet that may be, for surely there is no
Mortal who burns in Lucifer's domain,
Who suffers torment there, or grief, or pain,
Like to the least of mine. Yes, that I know.
Therefore I often wish I were not born
Or that I could not feel or understand
Since I can find no path that leads away,
And have no hope except this hope forlorn
That the time prophecied is now at hand
When Antichrist will come, and the last day.

Eo ho sì tristo il cor di cose cento

My heart so sad is in a hundred ways,
A hundred *ways* I would that I could die,
Since only if I *die* could I have peace,
Who have no *peace* save when asleep I lie.
But when asleep I *lie* I know such pain
That I of this great *pain* can have no cure,
Yet she could find a *cure,* were she not slow
To change, who, being *slow,* doth make me sore.
Yea, I am *sore,* by all the faith that's mine,
Since all that's *mine* no other thing can be
Than thing that both distasteful *be,* and ill,
So *ill,* indeed, it maketh me repine.
That I *repine* all I encounter see
Who *see* no way my heart with joy to fill.

23.

Me' mi so cattivegar sù 'n un letto

Upon my bed I toss as I opine
No other man who walks on two legs does,
Dreaming that I might hear: "The world's wealth's thine!"
If 't were, this way my fortune I'd dispose:
I'd see to it that my two arms would twine
For my delight the one toward whom goes
My heart and soul and body — all that's mine —
Eternally, nor surcease ever knows.
But since of those same things I have not one
— Those things I would I had ten thousand fold —
Each day, for woe a thousand deaths I prove.
My blood's in turmoil. Madly does it run.
It seethes as do a brook's wild waters cold.
I swear I'll make an end of being in love.

Thomas Caldecot Chubb

Da po' t'e'n grado, Becchina, ch'i muoia

Now that, Becchina, you long for me to die,
That I live long, not even God can desire.
Yet, dear my soul, I will not die gladly.
That would too greatly joy your scurvy sire —
Benci, I mean, a leathermake he.
For that alone my dying I'd bewray,
And not because life's anything to me.
Nay, but for him, to Christ for death I'd pray.
That my laments fall upon desert air,
Let it please them who hating me find good
For they'll spew poison till they know me dead:
Mita, Torella — hear them laugh and sneer —
And Nello and Pogges' — all of that brood
Except the one that was in Pisa bred.

25.

— Becchina mia! — Cecco, nol ti confesso —

"Becchina mine!" *"Cecco, I am not thine!"*
"But I am yours!" *"Now that I do deny!"*
"Then someone else's!" *"Not a fig care I!"*
"You do me wrong!" *"Send bailiff to collect the fine!"*
"I'll send a madam!" *"I'd split her head condign!"*
"Who'll split whose head?" *"That you will shortly see!"*
"You'd be that mean?" *"I would — to enemy!"*
"I'm not an enemy!" *"So you opine!"*
"Please don't tell lies!" *"I say the devil take you!"*
"You wouldn't like it!" *"Why? I want to know!"*
"You're too kind-hearted!" *"Not to you — this year!*
"If I were other?" *"Then happy I would make you!"*
"It's a shame that I knew you!" *"You're not lying now!"*
"Now no one can save me!" *"I won't try, no fear!"*

E' non è neun con cotanto male

There lives no man on earth without such pain
That he would not most gladly change his state,
Yet in me sorrow is so sovereign
No other wretch there is has woes so great.
For look, she thrusts at my most vital vein,
She whom I do adore. She makes me bleed.
She holds me as a vile and worthless weed.
To this my sins have brought me — this my fate.
Yea, she does say, has said, and say she will,
And ever since I spoke to her my love:
"You are indeed my mortal enemy!"
Therefore such agony my heart does fill
That I can only pray to God above:
"Lord, strike me blind — but take this love from me!"

27.

Lo mi'cor non s'allegra di covelle

My heart does not find joy in anything
I look upon or I hear men declare.
Noisome to me's become the very air
I breathe, such ill news does my lady bring.
Even the stars, she says, whose wandering
Is far above, would sooner be my own
Than she'd so bow herself that, grovelling,
She would allow me to touch the soles of her shoon.
Wherefore I call death life and far less woe,
For I would rather die once and for all
Than die a thousand times and yet live still.
O sonnet, to my lady, therefore, go,
And say that could I yesterday recall,
With ten-lashed whip I'd scourge her with good will.

Thomas Caldecot Chubb

28.

Sonetto, da poi ch'i' non trovo messo

Sonnet, since I cannot find messenger
To go to her for whom my heart doth long,
I'll thank you in God's name that you flight there
On my behalf confidently and strong,
And say to her that I will die of love
Except she show to me kind courtesy.
Yet, when you tell her this, oh stand aloof.
Even toward you I would feel jealousy.
But if she will accept me for her slave —
And that is far beyond my wildest dreams —
Promise her truly, say to her from me
That all that to a knightly soul beseems,
I do for her if only loyally
She'll show my woes the pity that I crave.

29.

Anima mea, cuor del mi' corp', amore

My soul, my body's heart, my dearest love
Have mercy upon me, have pity on me, I pray,
For in such sorrow I now live alway
That every hour I think my heart is rove.
I tremble in my grief. Love's wounds I feel,
And I wear bandages to ease their pain.
If I should die, small honor would you gain.
Death is an ill, an end, you could not heal.
Yet though I be not worthy to receive
Your pity and your kind sweet courtesy,
Still will I never weary in my prayer.
Love doth command and wish — believe, believe —
That every lover must love devotedly
Her whom his heart goes out to, his lady fair.

30.

— Oncia di carne, libra di malizia

"For every ounce of flesh, a pound of spite!"
So say you, but you know it is not truth.
Have you gone daft? Coin plentiful and bright
Ne'er's gained from one who bargain aye pursu'th.
With words you cannot pierce my heart — or quite.
The worse you speak, the more I hope for ruth.
No man will ever bend me to his might,
Or if man does, 't will not be you, i' sooth.
But I see well that you do spill forth love,
And therefore to your speech I pay no heed,
For your heart is love-smitten. That is clear.
You still sing that old song though false it prove.
A plague upon you then! Be this decreed!
To which I add — Good day, good morrow, dear!

31.

S'i' potesse d'amico in terzo amico

If I as friend to third friend openly
Could tell my lady, and still with honor to her,
How my heart feels, who am her servitor,
In such a manner that her enemy
My words would not be, then most sure it is,
If she but knew this, her love would I have,
And if I did, her virtue I'd preserve
Even in that place which 'neath her navel is.
Alas, then why so low do my thoughts fall
That I can win salvation in no way
Except I kiss her face and eyes and all?
Helen to her is like a muddy stream,
That's why. She makes Messina's light to gleam
With emeralds and rubies. So I say.

Thomas Caldecot Chubb

Se 'l cor di Becchina fosse diamante

If my Becchina's heart were diamond,
And all the rest of her were hard as steel,
Cold, too, as January in those lands beyond
The rising of the sun, which no heat feel;
If she had a fierce ogre for her sire,
Not genial leather-working artisan,
And I cracked whip at asses to earn hire,
Still she ought not bring me such grievous pain.
For were she near enough to hear my plea,
And could I but find eloquence as well,
I swear she'd grant the boon for which I pray.
And when I cried: "You're life-long dear to me!"
And other things I do not wish to tell,
I am convinced she would not answer nay.

33.

Se tutta l'acqua balsamo tornasse

If the world's waters became fragrant balm,
And the whole earth great carloads of rich gold,
And all this He would put into my palm,
The One Who in His hands all power doth hold,
If I'd agree my lady should know harm
And should depart the world, I'd tell him bold:
"Keep you these gifts. For me, they hold no charm,
But if she dies, let death me too enfold."
For I — unless perchance she did consent —
Would not permit hurt to one hair of her head
For all the treasure a thousand camels could bear.
Would God she knew this, knew that I had spent
Full many an evening, many a morning on her.
It was time wasted, lost, gone, vanishéd.

34.

Figluol di Dio, quanto ben avre' avuto

It would be good indeed, by God's own son,
If my dear lady love would only deign
To buy me for her slave like many a one
By corsair captured and then sold in chain.
Woe's me, my jailor's crueler, crueler far!
For I do swear, and would on holy fane,
That if she saw me dragged to where graves are,
"Who is that corpse?" she'd ask in great disdain.
None the less, Love, abide with her, I say,
For then I still may hope and not dispair,
Nor need my song be whistling in the dark.
Though she hate me as Siena hates Collé,
I'll humble myself — I know I can, I swear —
Until in her cold heart I strike a spark.

35.

I'ho sì gran paura di fallare

I have so great a fear of being amiss
Toward her, the gentle lady I adore,
I dare not ask the joys that I long for,
Yea, and with all my heart and soul, I wis,
And yet my heart assures me that so great
In her is kindness and sweet courtesy
That nothing I can do or say or be
Could make her who now rules me wax irate.
Oh, if my fortune made her but consent
That I should have from her such courtesies,
No lover would know greater happiness.
Go, sonnet, then; ask pardon on bent knees
For aught I say to her that doth displease,
Else will I live my days out in distress.

Thomas Caldecot Chubb

Deh, bastat' oggimai, per cortesia

You've said enough! I beg you no more speak!
To catch your breath, it's surely time to try!
It's true that Love could grant the thing you seek —
That is, if a fat capon could flutter and fly!
Soul of my soul, such cruel words why blurt?
Wish you I leap from cliff and meet my end?
You'll make me do myself some dire, strange hurt —
What 't is I know — if your ways you don't mend.
Would God you had already — that's my prayer!
For then indeed my heart would leap up high
Since I no more could ever bring you ease.
Why are you not as kind as you are fair?
Unless I do decieve me mightily,
You'd then say: "Take me! Have me! And so find peace!"

Io sono si̇̀ altament innamorato

I am in love so very loftily,
Ensnared by Cupid and my lady fair
I would not change my place, I do declare,
With any King or Emperor there be,
For I do love one, as you must agree,
Whom God gave all befitting a noble heart.
Hence he who serves her truly, stands apart,
Born 'neath auspicious star, and fortunately.
Yea, she so kind to me and courteous is,
This gentle damsel who's so truly mine
That, by her grace, I've dared to kiss her hand.
And now I have the surest auguries
She'll grant — if hale doth keep me God Divine —
Ere long all I desire or I demand.

38.

Io ho tutte le cose ch'io non voglio

I have all of those things that do not please,
But not one of the things I truly want
Since even Becchina cannot bring me peace.
To write my grief a page were far too scant,
To set down all the grief that fills my cup.
Yes, in a furnace I am all burned up,
Remembering the gift she gave to me.
The stars that glitter in the sky of night
Were less — I should have starved for them instead! —
Than were the kisses that she pressed upon
My lips. She did this for no other wight.
It was June twentieth. Dawn. The dark had sped.
The year was twelve hundred and ninety one.

39.

Per ogni gocciola d'acqua, c'ha'n mare

For every drop of water in the sea,
A hundred thousand joys to me have come,
And each of these brought greater joy to me
Than did Christ's kerchief to the men of Rome.
For know this, that by words and deeds I clomb
Into the topmost branches of Love's tree
And picked a flower there — to Love thanks be —
Mine now, who long had longed for its perfume.
But look you, when to earth I did come down,
I climbed again to garner the fruit too,
But could not. I was refused the thing I sought.
Would I'd content been with the flower alone,
Who now hath learned the proverb that all knew:
"Who seeketh all, oft endeth up with naught."

Thomas Caldecot Chubb

Se i' non torno ne l'odio di Amore

May my love never turn to hate of love.
I'd not have this though it won paradise.
In my heart dwells my lady in such wise
I would not ever chose another fate.
"Leave her two hours, and I'll make you emperor great!"
One said to me. My answer was: "Drop dead!"
For I, when I see her, am separated
From all thoughts that men call disconsolate,
And I, of all men, need and must not lack
Those things that make our woeful sorrows pass
Since I for sire have Brother Angiolier.
A thousand hours he's kept me on the rack.
Why? Ten years since I broke a worthless glass
And still I hear him curse at me and swear.

41.

A cui e in grado de l' Amor dir male

Let him who wishes to, of Love speak ill.
God will permit this, if his heart desire,
But I don't take that road, nor think I will
Who rather to say good of Love aspire.
No, it could never come to pass to me
That from this high opinion I did stray
Since Love the father is of courtesy
And he who knows Love far from evil will stay.
Indeed this Love so great a virtue hath
That even he who down the primrose path
Would wander, and would wander wickedly,
From sin to virtue turns at her behest
And lives thereafter well and honorably.
And most of all, Love makes a good man the best.

42.

Qualunque ben si fa, naturalmente

Whatever virtue in this world there is,
Love brought it forth as fruit is born of flower.
It makes a weak man strong, it gives him power.
None is so brute its metamorphosis,
Changing him from himself incredibly,
Cannot rain radiant beauty on his head.
Wherefore I swear to you, and fervently
He who loves not, far better had been dead,
Nor can a man do wonders without worth,
And worth is born of Love, and Love alone.
That I have told you, and now say again.
Haste then, my sonnet, straightway get you gone
To all the lovers that there are on earth,
And that Becchina made you, tell them plain.

43.

Chi non senti d'amor, o tant' o quanto

Who never has loved little or loved much
In whatsoever span of life he's found,
No right has to be buried in holy ground.
He's unrepentant usurer. Treat him as such.
Yea, he can boast, he can say vauntingly
That God and saints hate him with a fierce hate.
But he who loyally wears love's livery,
He can proclaim: "I am most fortunate!"
For Love so noble is beyond disdain
That did he lodge him in Hell's lord's own heart —
He in whom no peace is, nor should have been —
He would no longer feel eternal pain,
But rather feel the same joy that doth start
In the rude peasant when the Spring comes in.

Thomas Caldecot Chubb

44.

Becchin' amore, i' ti solev' odiare

Becchina love, one time I did hate you
As much as I with whole heart love you now.
Cecco, if I could only know you true,
My heart would be your servant, that I vow.
Becchina love, I challenge you to essay
To prove whether I false or faithful be.
Cecco, my Cecco, once again I say:
Prove that you're loyal. I'll your servant be.
Becchina love, now certainly I know
You do not want my worship of your worth
Since the impossible you postulate.
Cecco, your humbleness has moved me so
That in my soul I'll have no joy henceforth
Unless by your deed I am nine months great.

45.

Sed i' avess' un sacco di fiorini

Suppose I had a sack of florins bright,
Fresh from the mint, unclipped, and of full weight,
And Archidoss', and Montegiuovi's height,
And fifty mules with golden eagles for freight,
Still would it seem my purse but thrupence held
Without Becchina. Why chastise me, then,
Father? It easier were — let this be spelled —
To turn into a Christian the Saracen.
For I, as long as I do live, not die,
From this, my firm conviction, will not range,
That she — she is the earthly Paradise.
Would you have proof? Give heed to my reply.
He who but looks intently in her eyes,
From bent old man into a youth will change.

Io potrei così disamorare

I could less easily my love give o'er
Than from Bologna see Fucecchio's wall
Or from deep Pugna look on India's shore,
Or from Boccheggian' watch the slow sea crawl
Or look on, when I wished, the Sudary,
Or change to rogue one who despises all sin,
Or tell you what the meanings of dreams be,
Or make what already is never have been.
Therefore, why waste your time chastising me?
Unless I change at heart, it is no change
As I — believe you me — full oft have learned.
He who reproves me acts most foolishly.
Reproof but makes love's hot fires leap and range
Until a thousand times worse am I burned.

47.

La mia donna m'ha mandato un messo

This message has my lady sent to me:
Let naught betide but that I go straightway
To her, and by the very shortest way,
Yet not so swift I do me injury.
She says that her heart beats so urgently
That ere at sunset pales today's last glow,
She'll die — such is the joy she has in me —
Unless that I am I, unchanged, she know.
These are the tidings that to me are brought.
But can I do it, Lord, I beg you state,
Who three days journey from her am, and now?
I have no horse. I cannot go on foot
More than four miles a day. Beshrew my fate!
How can I help her? Dear Lord, tell me how!

Thomas Caldecot Chubb

48.

Sed i' avesse un mi' mortal' nemico

If I should have indeed a mortal foe,
And saw him trammeled in Love's signory,
Straightway he would become my friend, I know.
I'd serve him as my lord on bended knee.
You say I would not? That I do deny!
And why? Because this sorrow I too have known
Which in compare makes ragged beggary
Seem like the joy of emperor on his throne.
Let he who doubts this, my hard fate essay,
Who, for my sins, for five wild years and long
Storm-tossed have been upon Love's briny deep.
Then, when toward port at last I made my way,
Behold me driven back by current strong
Like those that past Messina's lighthouse sweep.

49.

Il comè nè'l perché ben lo sa Dio

Nor how nor why the good Lord does not know
That I no longer have the potency
To make Becchina give her heart to me
Though one time we were one who now are two.
Ah now I seek no other thing to do
Than find my grave and in it lay me down.
The devil's made me stubborn — that I own —
Who would forget but cannot. This is true.
I do believe that it is for some sin
That God has led me down into the slough
Of loving her by whom love is denied.
It's long — long, long indeed — that this has been.
So could I but my own love turn aside,
I know who I would scorn, and that's enough.

50.

Se io potesse con la lingua dire

If I could put in words but the least blow
That I was ever given by Love's hand,
And if my lady would but listen to my woe
Though she were cruelest one in all the land,
I say not even death whom all must know
Were surer than that she, all cruelty gone,
Would be that heart's desire I long for so,
Hearing my tale of grief, go on and on.
Oh, I would gladly bow the knee again
If my thus serving her would bring her bliss,
But I know well she is not so inclined.
She's sworn on oath, I've heard her swear it plain,
That if I ever come to where she is,
She will flee, seeing me. She will be gone with the wind.

51.

E' fue già tempo che Becchina m'era

It once befell that my Becchina was
So kind of heart to me I was content,
Nor did I need fair breezes and calm seas.
Her face alone brought joy incontinent.
But then, bad luck, I munched another pear,
And this brought so much torment, and straightway,
The woes of those in Hell far lesser were
A hundredfold than mine in every way.
Indeed I choked so on this fall from grace
That would I'd sealed my throttle up, and tight,
So that I could not swallow a mouthful at all
And never come then to so sad a case.
He speaks the truth who says — yea, he is right —
Who harms himself, himself must pay the toll.

52.

Becchin' amor! — Che vuo' falso tradito?

Becchin', my love! *What want you, false traitor?*
Your pardon. *You deserve it? Answer me!*
Well then, your pity! *You're humbler than before.*
And will be always. *Your security?*
My word of honor. *That you are without.*
Not toward you, dear. *There you go again!*
What did I wrong? *I know — of that no doubt.*
Tell me then, love! *Soon to you 't will be plain!*
You wish my death? *It could not come too soon.*
What cruel words! *I learned from you that song.*
Then I will die. *Do! It would be a boon.*
May God forgive you. *Still here? Get along!*
Would that I could! *Well, am I keeping you?*
You keep my heart. *And I will wound it, too!*

53.

Da Giuda in fuor, neuno sciagiurato

From Judas on, ne'er wretch unfortunate
Was, nor in a hundred thousand years will be,
Whose woes within a thousand miles of me
Brought him, and all because it was my fate
One to adore and love, whose heart was great
Only in deceits, betrayals, and treachery,
And yet St. John served Christ less loyally
Than her I served, than her I venerate.
Ah, the false innate nature of womankind!
It must be, always is, unfair, unjust.
Eve was the first. Eve wrote the irrevocable laws.
Wherefore, I know with all my soul and mind,
I have no choice. Grovel indeed I must,
Since she for her sad ways has this great cause.

The Sonnets of A Handsome & Well Mannered Rogue

27

54.

Qualunque giorno non veggio 'l mi' amore

Comes there a day I do not see my dear,
Then night like a fell serpent wraps me round
Until my head spins like a top unwound
So great the pain that in my heart I wear.
It seems a hundred thousand hours it were
"When comes the dawn? When will I see it?" I cry.
My tears drench me. I am nowhere dry.
Nothing there is can lessen the grief I bear.
Yet she has so changed toward me her esteem
That when at last I come to her city,
She looks at me and says: "What? Here so soon?
Knew you not that of someone else I dream?
A thousand times I love him more than thee,
Fly off! Fly off then! That would be a boon!"

55.

Lassa la vita mia dolente molto

Alas! How filled with grief my life has been!
I'm born, I swear, only to know distress.
From me has vanished all my joyfulness,
So rooted out it will not come again.
For look! I sow, another gathers in,
And if I'd comfort me, I lack the power.
A death's head is my face. Her heart doth dower
Death too to me, unhappiest of men.
Indeed, no other hope than Death have I
For Death alone could heal me of my woe
And of my unbending and unbearable pain.
Yea, it would be new life if I could die
Unless that news were brought — what news you know! —
Which set me free who long in prison have lain.

Thomas Caldecot Chubb

Maladetta sie l'or e'l punt' e'l giorno

Now curses on the hour, the minute, the day,
The week, the month, and on the hapless year
In which my lady falsely did betray,
And no more in my heart was sojourner,
And thus so wrapped it round without, within
With evil, anger, heart-sickness and dispair
That it were better, less woe had it been
If I fell into furnace, and burned up there.
For lesser is a pain with a known end
Than pain unending, though all pain is ill,
And so to have less pain, that pain I'd take.
I say this, but "Upon my soul", append,
"If, if I did not fear the pains of Hell,
I'd hang myself, and end of all pain make."

57.

I' m'ho onde dar pace e debbo e voglio

I could, and would, and should unto my soul
Bring peace. That is, if I had any sense!
Now that that fellow's filched from me my role,
Why should I mourn? Far rather let joyance
Be now my jerkin, sorrow not my stole.
It's my advantage Love has met an end
So let my cry to him: "Hail Lord! Hail friend!"
Then watch to ground not on another shoal.
That on this one I might ground I did fear,
Thinking about it all night and all day
Until it was a dart that thrust deep in.
And made me hate myself and no one more.
Now I want wife as I hate gaity and joy.
Ere she betrayed me, I did not even then.

Io vorre' 'nanzi'n grazia ritornare

I would I could return into the grace
Of that fair lady who lordship has of me.
Yea, to come back again to that dear place,
I'd turn from a river that bore gold plentifully.
No heart there is could dream what joy there'd be,
No heart how light and gay would be my breath.
Yet when sans love I live life drearily,
I am like one who hastes his steps toward death.
But I myself can blame myself alone.
It's I who made my days dismal and dire
Since, coward, I feared to strike her husband down
Who treats her worse than treated me my sire.
Ah me! Woe's me! So mean my heart's thus shown
That all who hear me laugh and call me clown.

Becchina, poi che tu mi fosti tolta

"Becchina, since you have from me been ta'en —
Two years ago, it seems a century! —
My soul has been enfolded gloomily
With anguish and with sorrow and with pain."
"Cecco, I swear to you that much more great
Had been my pain if I had aught to say.
Judge if I'm right, who left me to my fate.
The fool who won me, why did you not slay?
"Becchina, oh how could I? My tender soul
Would not permit that one who had known joy
With you, whatever be the cause, I kill."
"Cecco, if you a city rich as Troy
Should give to me — and now you know the whole —
I would not lift a hand to end your ill."

Thomas Caldecot Chubb

Ogn'altra carne m'è'n odio venuta

For every kind of meat I have disgust
Save one, and only one, I love full well,
And love it more each day I surely must.
Faugh! If it's not mine, may God go to Hell!
But now they tell me that it has been sold
Which drives me mad who long for it sans cease,
And that unless I spend great sums of gold,
I cannot have of it the smallest piece.
Hence I, the man who should make this bargain,
Who understands what she wants to be hers,
Do now speak other words than love's, I fear.
God knows how my poor heart is stabbed with pain
Because bright florins do not bulge my purse.
Then I could say those things she longs to hear.

61.

L'altrier sì mi ferìo un tal ticca

I had a sudden whim not long ago
To hasten to my love with swift good will,
And there I found her pacing too and fro.
Like a she-bear she seemed, nor could stand still.
But, seeing me, she thought that cure of ill,
Riches, was hers. "You have gold in your purse?"
She cried. I answered: "No!" I hear her shrill:
"Then hang yourself!" And that without remorse.
She was as prickly as a chestnut husk,
But then I showed her one coin tarnishéd.
She laughed. "What's this?" She cried. "Some trick you do?"
And fawned on me as sweet and soft as musk.
I could have led her with the thinnest thread,
But I went off, nor spent a copper sou.

Credenza sia, ma si'l sappia chi vuole

Here is a secret. No, let all folk know
That to Becchina I have given a gift
Of such a sort I dared hope to make shift
Tomorrow or tonight to escape from woe.
Yet, even at that, things are not what they were,
Thanks to God's power, lofty and divine
Which from my heart has pluced the thorny spine
Whose pricks are sharp as violets fragrant are.
I mean the spine that Love is called by men
Though they who call it this should go to school,
And when they do this, should learn something there.
Spine without rose, I say and say again,
As those who have been pricked by it can swear.
I speak the truth in this. I do not fool.

S'i mi ricordo ben, i'fu' d'amore

If I remember, Love once ruled me so
I was the most enamored man there was.
A year it seemed, did but two hours pass
Away from her — so filled I was with woe.
And she who was my lord and lady — lo
She gave me hope. She did not stand apart.
And one day, of the pity in her heart,
She gave me that last gift I longed to know.
But look what my bad fortune brought to me.
I went away, and now she is no more
Bewitched by me, nor I bewitched by her.
But oh what joy and pleasure it would be
If I could be as I was once before,
But now a hundred times less my longings are.

Thomas Caldecot Chubb

64.

Sed i' fossi costretto di pigliare

If I perforce to take the choice were made
Between hellfire and the woes of love,
And hesitated, my sins, I'm afraid
Would never be forgiven by God above.
For I do not think nor do I believe
That one could be by sorrow sorrowed more
Than I have been, who, loving her, so grieve
That I fear Love, whose hurt has been so sore.
But if I found I must needs love anew,
I would make pact with Love, having grown wise
That he must guarantee to keep me free
From her who long ago so cruelly slew,
And that I would not once more be her prize.
If not, I'd shout aloud: "It's Hell for me!"

65.

Qual uomo vuol purgar le sue peccate

He who would make amends in purgatory
For sins as great as those were of Judas,
Let him but fix his heart upon some lass
And have her love another incontinently.
If this does not dry up his vitals, kill,
— Her showing him such hateful cruelty —
You, sirs, can thrust a naked sword in me,
And after, turn and twist it as you will.
Perchance you'll ask me then: "How have you found
That this is so?" My answer: "My own woe!
I love a trull who, to my grief, alack,
Has dealt to me so many a grievous wound
That I no greater suffering would know
If I lay stretched and tortured on the rack."

The Sonnets of A Handsome & Well Mannered Rogue   33

Io combattei Amor ed hol morto

I have made war on Love, and him undone,
But that I made this war, I am contrite:
Though he was wrong, and I was in the right,
'T were better I were conquered, he had won.
He swore to bring me safely into port,
But the winds veered, he hurled me on beam's end.
If to shrewd tricks I did not then resort,
He would have falsely shipwrecked me past mend.
But ere, contesting him, I gained the day,
I could not so outwit him or his skill
That I did not sustain full many a blow
That well nigh slew me, took my life away.
But now that's over. Now he's worthless, nil.
I have escaped and he to death must go.

66.

Io sent' o sentirò ma' quel, d'Amore

Naught do I know of Love, and I would not,
More than he knows who has not yet been born,
But I do not deceive myself, I'm sworn,
To say than lover's mine's a happier lot.
For liberty is more to me than rule.
I'd rather live at peace than live in pain.
And when I was in love, I tell you plain,
Of grieving and of woe my cup was full.
But now all's laughter, all is laughter and song.
I do not know what melancholy is
Such joy I have now Love has gone from me.
O ye who a good road would walk along,
And, still alive, on earth know paradise,
Heed me, and be Love's mortal enemy.

Thomas Caldecot Chubb

68.

I' sono innamorato, ma non tanto

I am in love but not so utterly
I could not without thought cast Love aside.
I praise myself for this. I take great pride
That Love I've not made wholly lord of me.
Enough it is that I am gay and sing
For him, and serve as I Love's servant were.
To overpass such bounds is worth nothing.
My boast then: Love will not be my ruler.
Therefore, do not let any lady there is
Deem I will be her leige as many are
Though she is full of beauty and of grace.
Loving too much makes men plain fools. Hence this
I will not ever do, but stay afar
From that which the heart changes, and the face.

69.

Cara mi costa la malinconia

Dearly has cost me my deep melancholy
Since to forget it, and myself console,
The sinful, shameful art of usury
I have been driven to practice, body and soul.
But that is not by far my unhappiest role,
But rather when I love whole-heartedly,
I pick one who knows less — nor part, nor whole —
Of love than Mino of astronomy.
Yes, I have loved many, and again and again
And not one could have been a bit more chill
If she had been a hag a hundred years old.
Now I love one whose beauty makes me thrill
But I would stake my ears that she's so cold
That in the summer she has a chillblain.

E' non ha tante goccie nel mare

More drops there are not in the salty sea
Than times I have repented with whole heart
I did not take the flower that tenderly
She deigned to offer, who's so far apart
And far beyond all others that the Lord,
When he made her, needed make no other thing.
"Your love deceives you!" He who says such word
Should look on her and hear her sweet speaking.
For his indeed would be a heart of stone
Who came from her and had not fallen in love
And therefore said: "Cecco, your sonnet lies!"
A face more dear than hers is, has no one.
Her beauty all other beauty is above.
Not come yet has her like from Paradise.

Or se ne vada chi è innamorato

The man whom love has snared, knows naught but woe.
He well may say: "Accursed was the day
My mother bare me, gave me mortal clay;
Accursed the day my father got me too!"
I speak thus who have this to prove me true:
My woeful heart which felt love's bitter wound
In an ill-fated moment, has not known
Since then one hour in which ease it knew.
But there is worse to come, yea news that grieves
So greatly that I never can nor will
Have bleaker tidings ever brought to me.
'T would be the same for any man who lives
He whose love dies, and she a maiden still,
Will live his days out in black melancholy.

Thomas Caldecot Chubb

72.

Quando mie donn'esce la man del letto

Whenas my lady rises from her couch
At dawn, and had not put her make-up on,
There is not one so ugly, I avouch,
Who's not, compared to her, a paragon.
All beauty in her phiz has gone awry
Until she's searched and then daubed on, profuse,
Powder of gypsum, alum and ceruse.
Look at her and you get the evil eye.
But after she with fard has smeared her face,
There is not, seeing her, a man who lives
Who does not straightway fall in love with her.
Me too she has so tricked with these false ways
That for no other one I have a care.
It's thus that she to me chastisement gives.

73.

Tutto quest' anno, che mi son frustato

For one long year now have I put away
All of my vices saving one alone —
That's drinking — of the many I have known.
For this pray God forgive me as He may,
Who always when I wake at break of day
Have parched and salty gullet, dry as stone.
Who could refrain then — I am not the one —
From drenching tongue and palate? Who, I say?
Yet, at that, I bib only vintage wine
For sour country stuff makes my face wry
As does my lady when she scorn hath shown.
Then be my friend, and serve the grape divine
That dawn to dusk I may live riotously
Nor say one word I later would disown.

74.

I buon parenti, dica chi dir vuole

The best of kinfolk — he will this disown
Alone who cannot have them — florins be.
They're brothers and they're cousins certainly.
They're father, and they're mother, daughter, son.
By them alone reproach is never won.
They bring you raiment fine, sumpter and steed.
Before them French, Italians both bow down.
Baron and knight and scholar pay them heed.
They fill you full of zeal and hardihood
With wit to turn all fancies ever bred
To fact — bred now or fancies bred before.
Therefore you should not cry: "I've noble blood!"
If you've no coin in purse, but say instead:
"I'm as frail toadstool is when wild winds roar!"

75.

In questo mondo, chi non ha moneta

In this sad world, the man who has no pelf
Might just as well, indeed must needs impale
Himself upon a spit, or hang himself.
If he's that wise, his creditors will fail.
But he who has his bushel or his peck
Filled to the brim — and that, sirs, is not me —
Need swink no more, can hold his toil in check,
He who to win gold would even write poetry.
Yea, he who has — which I do not — great wealth
Out of his ample holding — this I say —
Can walk the road from sickness unto health,
And win himself worth and nobility.
Goodness is his, and wit and courtesy.
If I speak false, God strike me down today.

Thomas Caldecot Chubb

76.

Così è l'uomo che non ha denaro

The man who has no money in his purse
Is like a bird with feathers moulted away.
All turn from him. They will not say: "Good day!"
But shun him as they shun the plague or worse.
The sweetest apple bitter seems or tart,
And all he sees and hears distasteful is.
None's so polite to show him courtesies.
His life's an age in which he walks apart.
There's but one remedy will cure his ill
Which is to drown himself, and that forthwith,
For death than life stands him in better stead.
But he whose wallet good and true coins fill,
Why, all men tell him: "You are to me like bread!"
His wishes ring true like hammer of blacksmith.

77.

Se l'omo avesse in sè conoscimento

If mortal man were given insight clear,
He would most firmly bid Love stand aside
Unless to grant the least wish of his dear,
He were with all a lover needs supplied:
Florins, that is, many and gold and bright,
And jewels that he could give most generously
If it should be that they should please her sight
And make her treat him not disdainfully.
For he must able be to stand, proud, gay,
Nor fear the pointed finger and the scorn,
Nor that his rivals make of him a jest.
Let him love, then, or heiress or baseborn,
Nor middle road take. 'T is the only way,
For these will think that all he does is best.

The Sonnets of A Handsome & Well Mannered Rogue   39

Or udite, signor, s'i' ho ragione

Now listen, sir, and say that I'm no fool
To hang myself with rope until I die:
Because I am enrolled in Poverty's school,
My lady does not think me worth a fly.
I know it, having made full many a try,
Alone and in a crowd, all to my grief.
Do I but say a word, and scornfully,
She flouts me as if I were a vile thief.
That is because I'm poor. Had I a sou
To clink in purse, this shame I would not know,
But she would bow before its dignity.
O florins, you could cheer me up, yea, you,
Who now, being poor, must from my lady go
Because she will not speak or look at me.

79.

Un danaio, non che far cottardita

A groat, poor wretch, is all I have in purse
And that won't buy me broidered robes, or quite.
Hence like a half starved bear I am, or worse,
Who licks his paws to sate his appetite.
Alack! I hold my life in such despite
I do not think it worth while to bewray
That my good luck from me has taken flight
And that all point who see me on the way.
What is there then, what is there left for me
But to buy rope, tough-woven, strong of strand
And forthwith hang myself by the roadside,
Thus dying all at once incontinently
The hundred thousand deaths I die each day?
Hell's fear, I swear, is all that hold my hand!

80.

Di tutte cose mi sento fornito

I surely have enough of all good things —
Save for a few for which I do not care,
Such as whole shoes or raiment fit to wear,
Or even rags to warm my shiverings.
And in my purse such lack of money chings
That men, I swear, would rather meet ten devils.
Yea, lords, I have as large supply of evils
As January has not flowerings.
Of dining on scant cheer I have a feast,
Of sleeping on foul sheets, soiled and awry,
Of gulping sorry food and sour wines.
These are my troubles, and they are the least.
To tell the rest of them I will not try.
A sonnet only has fourteen short lines.

81.

La povertà m'ha sì disamorato

My love has poverty so driven away
That if I saw my lady cross my path
I scarce would recognize her. By my faith,
Her name I doubt I could recall or say.
And so hard frozen is my honor's flame
That if I were insulted by the most
Vile and degraded churl the world can boast,
All he would have from me is: "What a shame!"
Indeed, on me who once lived gaillardly
It's played so many a sorry, scurvy joke.
I, when I see it, flee as from the stake.
Hence I would like to see indelibly
Written: "He who'd live like a plump cook,
'Gainst being poor must all precautions take."

82.

I'son si magro che quasi traluco

I am so lean that light well nigh shines through me —
I do not mean of person, but of purse —
And owe such a lot more than any owe me,
There's not a straw left that I could disburse.
My income's gone to wrack. To my great harm,
I've naught to give away, and less to keep.
True, I still have and hold my little farm.
Its fruit each year's so small I'd sell it cheap.
But 't is my fate, who bound am by love's thong,
And if I'd the world's gold, it would be still,
To spend and to go bankrupt in a day.
Would God I had the sense to not do wrong!
No use. Instead I strive and always will
To get my hands on more to throw away.

83.

A chi nol sa non lasci Dio provare

Him who's not known this woe, may God forfend
From having, with his little, to do much.
"How do you know it's woe?" you ask me. Such
My answer: "Of hard cash I'm near the end,
Yet my expenses soar into the sky,
And all because I live by honor's rule."
Then to myself: "What will you do, rash fool?"
"If wise you'll hang yourself until you die.
Don't wait until you've plunged yourself in an abyss
That more than death itself will bring you pain
As I know well who've traded in that store.
Three times a day I'm given proof of this,
Three times by my dire proverty am slain:
When I awake, when I eat, and when I snore."

In una ch'e' danar mi dànno meno

When I do find that little coin is mine —
And my supply is always very scant —
I am as weak as is twice-watered wine,
As cowardly as Tristram's valiant.
I walk among folk with my head bowed low,
And than a mongrel cur am more hangdog.
To gain some, there's no deed I would not do
By night or day. Then I'd be no more rogue.
But if by luck and fortune I have won
Yes, if by chance, there should stick fast to me
Some few of those things of which lack I knew,
Before I had them, they'd be well nigh gone.
I'm not the sort to lend at usury
Like greedy priests and greedy friars too.

85.

Quando non ho denar, ogn'om mi schiva

When I do not have money, all confound
Me, and their faces turn away
I can sing songs. The bagpipes I can play.
It serves me naught without that hard stuff round.
I'm like one by river's steep bank found
With none to help him cross it with his load,
Or like crude cargo by rough hands bestowed
In the ship's bilges. None want me around.
I choke and gasp and heave enormous sighs
Like Mongibello's smoking cinder cone,
Or like a starving wolf who finds no prey.
Nothing seems good and fair. Far otherwise!
For I'm without the one shield man has known
And evil guides my feet their wandering way.

The Sonnets of A Handsome & Well Mannered Rogue   43

86.

Ogni mie'ntendimento mi ricide

All of my best endeavors go amiss
When with hard cash my pockets are not filled.
I am distraught as man in prison is.
I cry: "By God, O Death, let me be killed!"
But when I've plenty, the world's laugh is gay,
And each one of my ventures turns out well.
Then I am brave as is a lioncel.
He is a fool who throws his gold away!
Yea, if that happy dawn should ever shine
When I had riches, you would have to be,
To cozzen them from me, than Merlin more sage.
I'd be close-fisted as a Florentine,
And would not spend more often than once an age.
A doit, for a month's needs, would answer me.

87.

I'son venuto di sciatta di struzzo

I must have been a gluttonous ostrich bred
Since for my hunger I joined a soldier band.
But now I've pawned my corselet to get fed
And my linked coat of mail, you understand.
But though not fussy with a turned up nose —
I root and guzzle as a porker does —
I find that when I've eaten up my clothes,
I still am broke. I'm worse off than I was.
My gorget is the one thing I have left
Though it has often brought me good drinking.
Still let it join my doublet and the rest.
My lance I will not speak of — from me reft —
But shield and helmet, that's another thing.
That turns my stomach. Get them back I must.

Thomas Caldecot Chubb

88.

In nessun modo mi poss'acconciare

Myself I can't persuade in any way
To set my heart upon economy.
Indeed, I am compound of such a clay
Just thinking of it takes all joy from me.
Rather I am in turmoil, wits astray,
As one is who first battles the wild sea,
And rage and fury at my poverty
Is all I have to sell or give away.
But why should I beat head against the wall?
I'm what I am as surely as all men.
Yea, by my faith, I swear it unto you.
Do this seem strange? It is not strange at all.
As it is true or false — let this be plain —
May my love faithful be, or be untrue.

89.

Per ogni oncia di carne che ho addosso

For every ounce of flesh my ribs support,
I wear a hundred pounds of misery,
Nor do I even know what joy may be.
My lady, you see, keeps me on rations short.
She makes me skin and bones with her tongue's sport.
She nags: "Be close. Practice economy.
Then only will I give you of coin a mort."
Would I were cast in ditch as deep as sea!
There's nothing that is blacker or more hell
Than this damned penny-pinching, that I swear.
I hate it worse than freezing winter rain.
How should we really live, if we'd live well?
Hear what the doctors of Salerno declare:
Do what delights you, then you'll ne'er feel pain.

90.

Con gran malinconia sempre istò

I am so wrapped and robed in melancholy
That there is nothing that can bring me cheer.
Ah me! But why I am's unknown to me.
If you can tell me, what it is declare.
Yea, waste no time, but let me have it plain
If that you can, since I cannot tell you
Who die each day a thousand deaths in pain.
If you can bring me solace, oh pray do.
For as I am, I could not suffer more,
And so, for God's love, give me counsel sage:
Tell me how I can be where once I was.
Enough if you do this. It's all I implore.
If not, immersed in gloom beyond assuage,
All I can do is mope and sigh: "Alas!"

91.

La stremità mi richèr per figluolo

Dame Poverty proclaims I am her son,
And I as Mother greet her loyally.
I was begotten out of woebegone
Sorrow; the nurse I had, Despondency.
My swaddling clothes were woven from the homespun
Rough fabric of vexation, grief imbrued.
From top of sconce to heels I have not known
Anything ever that you could call good.
Then, when I grew to manhood, for my ease
And consolation, I took myself a wife.
She talks from sun-up till the stars are lit.
A thousand guitars make fewer cacophanies.
Who takes a second if she leaves this life,
Has far less sense than has a grain of wheat.

Thomas Caldecot Chubb

92.

Per si gran somma ho' mpegnate le risa

All laughter I have put in pawn, I trow,
For such a great sum that it does not seem
It is a pledge I ever could redeem.
Pisa weighed out in coin were not enow.
Indeed gloom grips me so that I avow
I'd break my neck before the faintest smile
Did I let cross my lips the shortest while.
So have my spirits sunk, they have sunk low.
The other night I dreamed — a wild nightmare —
That I saw something and laughed fit to kill,
Whereat I woke and blushed with shame bright red,
And so said to myself: "Would God I were
One who could do whatever I might will.
Then he who laughed would surely lose his head!"

93.

I'ho si poco di quel ch'i'vorrei

I have so little of the things I want
I do not see how they could fewer be,
And I, in fact, might boast: Than me more scant
Of means there's no one I will ever see.
For I am one who, if I went to sea,
Do doubt one drop of water I would know.
My fortunes, then, must rise inevitably
Since there's no way that they could be more low.
Indeed, that's why to gloom I do not yield,
But do instead rejoice at all my woes
As the wild savage does, or so they say.
To cheer me, here's the argument I wield:
As once a wise man said to me who knows,
A day comes worth a hundred times today.

94.

Egli è maggior miracol, com'io vivo

That I'm alive is greater miracle
A hundred thousand times, it seems to me
Than it would be to see an olive tree
Ungrafted on its limbs bear pears as well,
Or that you'd wean a man from wickedness
With the same ease that he drinks thirstily
Since of life's dower of lovely gifts that bless
I have no more than a blind man can see.
Yet I have this small help. I never cease
To hope. 'T is hopes my contrite heart sustain
Or else a thousand times I'd surely died.
Though every day and hour my troubles increase,
There'll come a time when a new star will reign,
My bad luck turn to good luck undenied.

95.

L'uom non può sua ventura prolungare

Man cannot make his bad luck last more long
Or less long than is willed by destiny,
And so methinks that I will walk along
The path that nature has prepared for me.
Thus — if I can — I'll do my best to see
I do not add more to my melancholy,
And have to say that I've lost through my folly
Whatever pleasures that there still may be.
'T is true I've learned this lesson very late,
But not too late to find it conforting:
I've learned two ills are surely worse than one.
Hence I rejoice and look for better fate
For I am sure each day will something bring
That does not vex me, and till life is done.

Thomas Caldecot Chubb

96.

Se Die m'aiuti, a la sante guagnèle

If by the saints' and by Our Lord's good grace,
Were ended, from Siena, my exile,
I swear I'd let an enemy slash my face
And would rejoice with milk and honey smile,
I swear I'd seem a dove — a dove of peace —
So humble I would be and so contrite, —
I who have suffered such indignities
There's no one cruel enough to do such spite.
Yes, every evil I have ever known
Would be joy, could I have the hope, though frail
That patient penitents have in purgatory.
But no. So great have my misfortunes grown,
I will not in her dear streets stand nor dwell —
That's never — till my father is friend to me.

97.

Babb'e Becchina, l'Amore e mie madre

Love and my mother, Becchina and my sire
Have trapped me as a bird is trapped in lime.
My father first. Each day and many a time
He curses me and sends me to Hell's fire.
Becchina to such rare gifts doth aspire
Mahomet could not furnish them, nor find.
Love makes me love one who is so unkind
She must be Gaetto's daughter, who robs for hire.
And now my mother. She is all undone
Because she has not got the evil power
To do to me the hurt she longs to do.
One day I greeted her as should a son.
"Now," thought I, "now she will no longer lour."
"Begone!" her answer. "May a sword slay you!"

S'i' fosse foco, arderei 'l mondo

If I were fire, I would burn up the world;
If I were wind, with storms I would it sweep;
If I were water, I would drown it deep;
If I were God, to hell it would be hurled;
If I were Pope of Christians good and true,
I would rejoice I'd put all in confusion.
If emperor, know you what I would do?
I'd order of beheadings a profusion.
If I were dead, I'd flee before my sire;
If I were living, I'd run from him in shame;
And from my mother I would do the same;
If I were Cecco, as I am and was,
I'd take all pretty girls as fair as fire
And let the others have each ugly lass.

99.

Tre cose solamente mi so' in grado

Three things, and three alone, do I desire,
And none of them — woe's me! — is often mine:
Women and throwing dice and drinking wine.
These fill my heart up with a leaping fire.
But oh how seldom such joys I acquire,
And all for lack of money round and bright.
Thinking of this, my plaint is: "You poor wight!
Your empty purse forbids you to aspire!"
And then I say: "A dagger in his heart!"
I mean my father's who keeps me spare and thin.
No need to diet when I returned from France.
Than from his hands a single penny to win
Even in the generous season of Eastertide,
A crippled hawk to take crane has more chance.

Thomas Caldecot Chubb

100.

Qual è senza denar innamorato

He without gold in purse who falls in love,
Should make himself a gallows and hang betimes,
For he does not die once, but dies more times
Than did the one cast down from heaven above.
Now I, and for my sins, am such a one,
A wretch, if there were ever of this sort.
I even lack two pennies to hale to court
The enemy who wrong to me has done.
Why don't I hang me then, and end my tale?
One reason only, and it's vain, I know.
I have a rich, old father. He may fail.
And so I sit and wait for him to die.
But he'll live on until the sea is dry.
To torture me, God keeps him hearty and hale.

101.

Sed i' credesse vivar un dì solo

If I thought I would even live a day
Longer that he who sets my life awry,
Full many grateful thanks to Christ I'd say,
But that's as likely as that I could fly.
It is as likely as that Genoa's mole
Should topple, being butted by a goat.
Death's chill can never pierce to freeze his soul
Whose ill-gained riches are so warm a cloak.
My father is the one to whom I refer.
He takes the same joy in tormenting me
That saint in heaven does to see God's face,
So how can what I think so wicked be?
Yet all that Doctor Taddeo will aver
Is: "Age alone will lead him to Death's place."

102.

I' potre' anzi ritornare in ieri

Far easier could I return to yesterday
And in Becchina's favor be again,
Or into a flour a diamond grind away,
Or see a friar live in wretched pain,
Or belly grow like Min Pier's, I so lean,
Or on a scrawny drumstick myself sate
Than bring that fellow to fever and death — I mean
Sire Angiolari, demon incarnate.
If they still lived, Galen and Hippocrates
Would know less why this is than Donato — he
Who grammar wrote not medicine, I weet.
How can he ever die then, tell me please,
Who is so learnéd and built so ruggedly
That, like the ostrich, he can iron eat?

103.

I'ho un padre sì complessionato

I have a sire, and of such kidney he
That though he crams him with the sorriest fare,
He doth digest it as salubriously
As does another fat mutton or viands rare.
Yet I am such a fool, of sense washed free,
That if I see him gobble down but two
Ripe figs — I swear to you that this is true —
I have him started toward eternity.
Now, though, I've given up this fond idea.
Now, ere he dies, I think and firmly know
The long-lived owl to his own death will come.
Judge then if I should not shed many a tear.
Why lingers he? To him here's reason enow:
To keep a canting lay friar in our home!

104.

Merzè, merzè, se mi' prego t'è in grato

Wilt have me, Death, for I would thank you well
If one thing or the other you would do,
And if I think it neither good nor ill
When you have done it, then see to it you
That I, as many times from mangonel
As at Grosseto salt grains are, am hurled
And this is it — observe the thing I tell:
Take either myself or my father from this world.
For I can win no other thing than bliss
If you should slay me. It would be my gain.
Life is it, and not Death, to leave my woe.
But if you slay this robber, this Selvain,
Then this will happen, Death, then this, then this:
I'll roll in gold and to the baths I'll go.

105.

Sed i' avesse mille lingue in bocca

If in my mouth a thousand tongues I had
And each were made of tempered iron or steel,
And was with Fra Paglaio's speech arrayed,
From the life span I could not coax one thread
Of him who around living a guard hath spread
More strong that usurer does to guard his gold.
I mean than knight whom vair does not enfold,
That Fra Gaudente whom fever cannot strike dead.
Death, Death, herself, most greatly fears to die,
But if she came to him, I am most sure
She would expire, and he prove curable.
His hide's so tough that if unto the sky
One wished to build a tower, tall, secure,
To use him for foundation would be well.

The Sonnets of A Handsome & Well Mannered Rogue   53

106.

Il pessimo e'l crudele odio, ch'io porto

The terrible and the cruel hate I bear
For my own father, and that rightly too,
Will make him live as long as the wandering Jew
As for a long time I have been aware.
How I am wronged, O Nature, hark and hear.
The other day I begged for sour wine.
He had a hundred kegs, the Hebrew swine.
God's truth, I thought he'd kill me then and there.
"What if I asked for vintage rare and old?"
To test him, these shrewd words came from my maw.
The villain spat and straight into my face.
Yet some: "You should not thus despise him" hold.
If they but knew his faults and my disgrace,
They'd say instead: "You ought to eat him raw!"

107.

Non potrebb' esser, per quanto Dio fece

It must be true, by God who made the man,
That my sire's quaffed elixir of pure gold,
For he is like a bull in his élan,
And yet he is — or nearly — eighty years old;
Or else he has so glued to him his soul
With pitch it can't depart, it is not free
To live outside his body and be whole,
Yes, this it is forbidden utterly.
Withal, I think he's an unhappy wight,
And this I do not falsely swear to you,
Who deems there is no heaven nor aught up there.
Nor is my mother fortunate, poor sight.
I hear she's deep in trouble, she's in despair.
And so things go the way I want them to.

Thomas Caldecot Chubb

108.

Non si disperin quelli de lo 'nferno

Oh, let you not despair who live in Hell
For here is one who's 'scaped its lock and key,
And that is Cecco as you know full well
Who thought he'd dwell there through eternity.
But now the page is turned and in such wise
That from henceforth I'll only know great joy.
My father's left his hide — Angiolari dies
At last, who all year long brought such annoy.
O sonnet, to that other Cecco go
Who, in the monastery, does nothing but brood.
And say his sire, Fortarrigo, too is half dead,
Wherefore he should abjure all thought of woe
And cram his craw with this immortal food,
And longer live than Enoch and Elijah did.

109.

Chi dice del suo padre altro, ch'onore

He who says aught but good about his sire,
Should have his tongue sliced off with a sharp blade.
The deadly sins are seven, it is said,
And this the deadliest. No sin is more dire.
If I were priest or but a begging friar,
This plea before the Pope, I would have laid:
"Your Holiness, proclaim you a crusade
Against all those who thus earn heaven's ire."
And should I ever find one whose black sin
Had led him to such arrant wickedness,
I'd see him cooked and eaten not by men
But by fierce dogs and wolves, that ravening brood.
May God forgive me then in mercifulness.
Sometimes my words to mine were rustic and rude.

110.

Io son sì magro, che quasi traluco

I am so lean that light well nigh shines through me –
I do not mean of person, but of purse –
And have no friend or parent who would know me
Since now my garb is like a beggar's or worse.
And this is all I have that is of worth:
The starveling hope that someday I may thrive.
Even when my father walked upon this earth,
Me to such sorry state he did not drive.
Yet I could well be rich, and know the art.
My mother, Ciampolino, and Zeppa evilly
Have gained a mort, and from me came the most.
If what is mine, they would but yield me part!
Small chance! In swindling, they're a trinity
Like Father, Son, and like the Holy Ghost.

111.

Mia madre m'ha 'ngannat' e Ciampolino

My mother's cheated me, nor's Ciampolin'
In this had idle hands, I dare well say.
What's more, their joy and bliss would be most keen
If an assassin sped me on my way.
He, by the way, is such a vile poltroon
Even my lackey shakes not at his mien,
But when he robs me, it's another tune,
And one not written by St. Augustine.
Would they gave but one penny to me, one!
But she, my mother, gains her ends so well
My sack is empty, that of Mino full.
Indeed, I do not seem to be her son,
But stepson rather as I hear her tell.
And Mino eats the fruit I ought to cull.

Thomas Caldecot Chubb

112.

Mie madre disse l'altrier parol'una

My mother said to me the other day
A word which pleased me not immeasurably:
"If I have robbed you, snatched your coin away,
What care I? It means not a fig to me!"
To which I answered, choosing carefully
My speech: "Why do you injure me, why slay
Only to give to Zeppa, who, you say
Is Lucca's Holy Face. This confounds me.
The rogue is everywhere. Where he's unknown,
That place, that place, would God that I could find.
You know what I would do, for I am wise.
But that I cannot. He's stubborn as a stone."
Your answer: "Scratch your eyes out, and be blind!"
You're right. Then I'd not see his robberies.

113.

Su lo letto mi stava l'altra sera

The other day I lay upon my bed
And I pretended I was fast asleep,
When lo! I saw my mother toward me creep,
Her face with hateful malice torturéd.
Upon my couch she sprang as wild beast dread
And clutched me by the throat — I have not lied —
And tried to choke me until I was dead.
Had I not struggled free, I would have died.
Medea was less evil, who murderously
With her own hands her own son strove to slay
Than was my mother who my undoing thus sought.
Because I asked for what belonged to me
From Mino, she sought to ruin me and to betray.
Had I not, she'd have given me no thought.

Mie madre sì m'insegna medicina

My mother taught me to use medicine
Of such cruel kind it did not make me well.
She bade me eat — she hoped for my decline —
Eight or ten fishes for my morning meal.
These my interminable fevers would dispel,
Tertian and quartan would no more be mine.
She sang the praises of Chiana eel,
Than theriac more health-giving and fine.
Ox flesh she urged on me, onions with cheese.
The latter certainly would cure each ache
If I would only munch it gluttonously.
But if not one of these should bring me ease
˙And I was tortured till I thought I'd break,
Let me gorge oil-smeared salad, and I'd see.

Sì fortamente l'altrier fu' malato

I was so desperate sick the other day
That I had even lost the power to speak,
Whereat my mother to cure me did essay
To mix a brew so deadly and so quick
That me not only, but the vasty sea
It would have poisoned. She said: "Drink this now!"
But I made sign to her: "Not me! Not me!"
For not to drink it I had made firm vow.
To this, she answered me: "Yes, you will sir!
You'll drink it if I force it down your throat!"
Fear shook me out of silence as fear could,
And I cried out: "I'm well, and well you know't!"
I would not, and I will not take a drink from her —
Not if she drank it first to prove it good.

Thomas Caldecot Chubb

116.

Tant' abbo di Becchina novellato

Of my Becchina so much have I said,
And of my mother and father, and of Love,
That half the world I have well weariéd.
Now, therefore, I'll essay another stave.
For there is not a theme so fine and fair
It does not become stale with use and time,
And so — 't will please me, too — I now prepare
And send each gentle heart a different rhyme.
Yes, in my sonnet's sestet, I will try
To tell the whole of what I hold the truth,
And blessed indeed be he who understands:
I am so filled with rage that I could die
To see one rich who should live starved forsooth;
To see one starved when wealth should fill his hands.

117.

I' non vi miro perzar, morditori

You do not hit the mark, you backbiters,
When you prate loud that I will be like you
Who every day turn into every hue
Before what you have filched you put in purse.
Is this your true opinion, gentle sirs?
Think you because for sport I've gambled all,
I'll now turn canting friar — what could be worse?
I'll now not play for big stakes or for small?
Well, know you this, and may it bring heartbreak:
I've learned so well to think and do and say
That here and far from home plenty I have,
While you — and this is good news, no mistake —
Must die of shame, must die of shame each day
Because you have to rob and steal to live.

118.

Dugento scodelline di diamanti

Two hundred saucers brimming with the best
Bright diamonds would Lano for his own
Possess; twelve nightingales at his behest
To sing their songs for him with dulcet tone;
A hundred thousand sacks with besants full,
Each lady that he wishes, fair of looks;
Power to checkmate anyone he will,
Taking their knights with his advancing rooks:
And if he wishes, too, some heliotrope,
Well, let him have it, on whom I do heap
In words those many things which I can't give.
If he has sense — and this he has I hope —
As well as his good looks, these let him keep,
And as much more as he would like to have.

119.

Giugale di quaresima a l'uscita

Sharp-tasting tangy jujubes at Lent's end,
And plums in the first days of February,
And almonds new in January I send
To Lano, who is joy fulfilled to me.
For I do love him more with heart and mind
Than most love life, and he too swears I'm his.
This you could see even if you were blind.
I go to him — this nature's true law is —
As to a bar of iron goes lodestone.
Love doth command this — glad it does am I —
Because of his unequalled handsomeness
Which is so great I cannot set it down.
But of his virtue I must needs say less.
And of his sense, for if I did I'd lie.

Thomas Caldecot Chubb

Udite udite, dico a voi, signori

Give ear, give ear, my lords, to you I say,
And answer me, O you who lovers are,
Have ye seen one among their great array
Who love's three colors on his face doth wear?
He's pink, and he is white, and cramoisin.
But tell me now who stand before you here,
Will ever he so kind to me have been
That I those self same hues with him could share?
We think that you could never do this thing
For he will never change his feelings so
That he would bow to you with humble head.
If he does not, I'll fall in my grieving
To earth, and there begin to sigh in woe,
And in four days, I think, be buriéd.

121.

I' so' non fermo in questo opinione

To my resolve I cannot steadfast be,
That is, to love no more — and I swore this —
A man who showed me such great cruelty
Though for this cruelty there no reason is.
But I say this which no one can gainsay
That to not serving you I'll faithful be
Since as a crime my sweetness you bewray.
This do you, and without cause certainly.
Yea, since I now know that you do not know
Me longer, and to me are recreant,
Your service I forever do abjure,
Adding you are insane, your wit is scant
If you don't now repent — and that is sure —
And at the same time also have great woe.

Un Corso di Corzan m'ha sì trafitto

One Corso from Corzan's so wounded me
That nought avails the healingest herbs there are,
Nor medicines that sweet or bitter be:
Not theriac that comes from Egypt far.
I have read Galen's writings thoroughly
And in them nothing found to ease my pains.
They're like one drop of water in the sea
So deeply runs the poison in my veins.
Because of this I have grown desperate
Since no persuasion any power has.
To this port Love has brought me, my sails furled.
I live more shaken — that is my sad fate —
Than any man there is or ever was.
Who's wronged me, may God take him from this world.

123.

In tale, che d'amor vi passi'l core

Whenever that love lodges in your heart
Sir Corso, may it surely bring you down
Lower than trunk of statue overthrown.
Like poison in your veins be love's cruel dart.
And may it make you bellow night and day
As when he sees a bear doth bellow bull;
And as drunkard drinks down flagons full
Of wine mayst thou drink fire and woe, I pray.
And if restraint on me had not been laid
I'd as much evil say as this and more
Unto thy darling minion, winning and gay,
Who is the handsomest fellow ever made.
But love forbids which me hath smit so sore.
My mind's on him. I have no more to say.

Thomas Caldecot Chubb

124.

Da te parto 'l mie core, Ciampolino

My heart I've torn from you, O Ciampolino,
And if true friends we never seemed to be,
Now you and I are mortal enemy.
You've robbed me more of mine, even than Mino.
And when I ask it back, I hear your voice
Cry gutter style: "I don't get what you say!"
Know then: I can eat partridges or play
At dice, or cast my eyes upon young boys
As well as you, but I do now forswear
All three of these — all three! Then no one can
"Look at this pauper strut and swell!" declare.
But you — or so you say — you're quite a man.
Then let God give you health and days to spare,
And you will then boast: "Ha! It was Christ's plan!"

125.

Io feci di mi stesso un Ciampolino

I made myself another Ciampolino
Because I thought that I was dear to him.
Yes, in my soul we two had one become,
Though he loved Pier, Giovanni, then Martino.
But if he ever held me in his fee,
I now am far from his heart's market place,
Who diddled and deceived me utterly,
Nor even if a miracle took place,
If water turned to wine one pennyworth
I'd trust him. I once did, and that is plain.
Never mill sent me flour so pure white.
But then he wronged me, I swear by heaven and earth,
And treated me as if he were a Cain.
"He's fool who trusts a dice thrower!" I now write.

Se tu se' pr'e forte Ciampolino

If you are strong and valiant, Ciampolino,
You need to be, or so it seems to me,
For here comes Tesé as you plainly see,
The one you flouted at San Pelligrino,
And with him one, a very mastiff, strides.
Tell me then, Ciampolin', what will you do?
Set at the two and slice and baste their hides?
Or be a chicken-hearted coward, you?
For if you flee, you will be in disgrace,
But if you stand and fight with a high heart,
You will be praised as a most fearless man.
But I already see turn white your face.
To run away I think's your chosen part,
And at high speed, as long as you still can.

127.

Sì se' condott' al verde, Ciampolino

My Ciampolino, you are now so broke
That with your candle, you've burned candlestick,
And that's because your gambling is a joke.
At throwing dice, you haven't learned a trick.
Yet I gave you advice, and plenty too.
"Don't play with fire," I said. "It's very bad."
But not one word of wisdom stuck to you
Who do not have the sense that Merlin had.
And since I've found you somewhat dim of wit
The meaning of my words, I should make known:
The candlestick is a good simile!
You owe so much — and that's the truth of it —
That if into a ditch you are not thrown
Before May comes, in prison you will die.

Thomas Caldecot Chubb

128.

Quando'l Zeppa entra'n santo, usa di dire

When Zeppa went to church, he used to say:
"To Thee, Good morrow God, today I cry."
Then crossed himself. It almost made us die,
Each one of us who saw him act that way.
Thereat his sins so loudly would he pray
That all could hear them, and not God alone,
And when the time came that he got him gone,
Never a Jew, he'd sing some churchly lay.
Crossing himself, his gestures were so mad
That oft he put his finger in his eye.
It was a wonder no one killed him quite.
'Twas perhaps because Capocchio loved the lad,
Or that he pummeled Branca so furiously
That all men thought he was a sodomite.

129.

Boccon in terr'a piè l'uscio di Pina

Long after curfew, with his arms outspread
I saw Ser Mino kneel 'neath Pina's room
And I began to listen to what he said,
And could have till dawn drove away night's gloom —
That is, if he had breath to speak that long
The gabble and the chatter he'd begun.
"Let me come up! Let me come up!" his song;
The answer that she made to him: "Like fun!"
"At least, then, take this money, take this gold
You will seem fairer to me — even you —
With broidered slippers you could wear so well."
"I'm on my way! But wait a minute! Hold!
You would not give them thus if they were true.
Capocchio falsed them. Go — with him — to hell!"

The Sonnets of A Handsome & Well Mannered Rogue   65

Per cotanto ferruzzo, Zeppa, dimi

"Zeppa, are you so vile one puny blade
Can make you flee as if from hue and cry?"
"It can and does, I answer and reply.
Ho! Ha! Not good this answer I have made?"
"Good? Do you call it good to imitate
A whirlwind that spins off like fluffy gauze?"
"Better flee swift, say I, than that my late
Departure of great harm to me was cause!"
"Flee, then, nor let your glance turn back, lest he
Who's in pursuit should hurt you in my name
So sore its pain you could not well assay."
"My fleeing would not please you? Then woe's me,
Dear love! Yet none can cry 'Shame! Shame!'
No trifle 'twas that sent me on my way!"

El fuggir di Min Zeppa, quando sente

When Mino Zeppa sees an enemy,
He is more expeditious in his flight
Than Pier Fasteo, who, from oversea,
Flew to Siena in a single night.
Indeed, if I should tell you truthfully
His speed, you'd answer: "You exaggerate!"
O God, all things are possible to Thee;
Make Thou just once his running temperate.
From Lodi to Pavia, in one bound,
He goes. 'T is naught. He could bound back again,
So practiced he'd be scarcely out of breath.
Since babe in arms can make him flee, or sound,
I, to keep up, would gasp or pant in vain.
Yet hear him: "Sir, what frightens you to death?"

132.

Se tutta l'otrìaca d'oltre mare

If all the inflaming drugs from oversea
And all of Genoa's white and fiery wine
Were poured down Mino's throttle, Mino mine,
The one who's always Zeppa called by me
They could not warm his heart so glowingly
That he'd not flee to India, this proud
Appearing knight, if jousters suddenly
"Have at him, lads!" cried fiercely as they rode.
The jest is, though, he thinks that he is bold,
But me he would not ever give a scare.
Did he, my love would turn her face away.
He's like those Radi cowards in days of old.
I wonder if he knows that everywhere
Men follow him, and jeer: "Get on your way!"

133.

Per Dio, Min Zeppa, or son giunte le tue

By God, Min Zeppa, now the truth is out,
So if you can, defend you from its say!
You by a well-baked brick were hit such clout
Upon your pate, an ox 't would surely slay.
Being a man, of no more had you need,
And so not once but eight times, you sought peace.
Then hang yourself, lewd, filthy, drunken, mad,
And far more scorned than anyone there is.
Indeed, even if you had not the least shame,
You'd surely walk about with eyes cast down,
Nor would with other folk peringrinate.
Of rogues, you surely bear the oriflamme,
O son of one who does so itch, it's known,
That she has wearied all who fornicate.

134.

Se'l capo a Min Zeppa fu tagliato

If you should hack off Mino Zeppa's head
As dummy's is when jouster rides at tilt,
It would leap back in place — or so 't is said —
And he would be unharmed, with no blood spilt.
If you should hurl him in a mangonel
Like ass over city wall, he would not faint.
Not even a draught of poison can do him ill
Any more than to John the Baptist, now a saint.
Why is this so? Why is this God's own wish?
The reason: Death himself says, "I would scoff
At myself ere I would enter so foul an abode."
If you should bind him with an anchor rode
And cast him in the sea, he would swim off
Like Nicolo Pescé, become half fish.

135.

Lassar vo' io trovare di Becchina

I would my dear Becchina no more praise,
Dante, but would the puffed-up Captain exalt
Who shines like a gold florin though metal base,
Who looks like Caffa sugar but tastes like salt,
Who seems white wheaten bread but is coarse rye,
Who stands like tower but is pavement too,
Who is a kite but flies like falcon high,
A hen though he cries *cockadoodledoo.*
O sonnet mine, to Florence get thee hence
And tell the dames and damsels you find there
Their paragon is nothing but vain show.
Meanwhile a hundred tales of him I'll swear
To good King Charles, the lord count of Provence.
Annoy for what I say, the rogue shall know.

Thomas Caldecot Chubb

136.

Dante Alighieri, Cecco, 'l tu serv' e amico

Dante Alighieri, I Cecco, your servant and friend,*
Commend myself to you as to my lord,
And then I pray you by Love's god-like word
Who has your sovereign been time without end
That you forgive me words that might offend —
And that you will assures your gentle heart —
And what these are I now to you extend:
Your sonnet contradicts itself in part.
For as I read it, in one place you cry
The words too subtle are to understand
When your soul "I saw Beatrice" seems to say.
But then to your dear ladies this you sigh
"I understand full well!" So, in the end,
Yourself to your own words do give the lie.

*Sonnet 136 is in reply to this Dante sonnet in his
    Vita Nuova:

Beyond that sphere that widest circlest,
There goes a sigh that issues from my heart.
In it a new faculty, at weeping Love's behest
Planted, forever seeks the loftiest part.
When it doth reach the place of its desire,
It doth perceive a lady honored and praised,
Who shineth and with such effulgent fire
The pilgrim can but gaze on her amazed.
It seeks her such that when it telleth me
I cannot understand, so subtle its praise
Unto the heart that it to speak doth incline.
I know, though, that it talks of my lady,
For very often *Beatrice* it says,
And then I understand, dear ladies mine.

137.

Dante Alighier, s'i'sò bon begolardo

Dante, if I'm a nonsense-talking lout,
I don't surpass you. This I do declare.
If I eat stranger's food, you taste their fare.
If I munch fat, grease fills your starved mouth out.
If I cut cloth, why then you card the wool.
If I speak folly, foolishness you spout.
If I play lord, you are Sir Worshipful,
A Lombard lean, if I'm a Roman stout.
Therefore, praise God, it would be to deplore
If either of us should the other blame.
To do this would show little sense I vow.
That's all. But if you wish to argue more,
Beware, for I can put you quite to shame.
I am a gadfly, you a clumsy cow.

138.

Quando Ner Picciolin' tornò da Francia

When Nero Picciolin' returned from France,
He had so many florins in his purse
That most men seemed as poor as mice — to curse
Or sneer at in his haughty indifference.
He mocked at them in French: *"Mal chance, mal chance — "*
He meant bad luck — "has fallen on every one.
They're all such beggars I would be undone
If toward the best I turned my countenance."
Now — through such great good sense — he's fallen so low
That there is no one left not far too high
To give him the scant courtesy of a nod.
I'll stake my life against a florin or so
That when another eight months have gone by,
For but a crust of bread, he'll say: "Praise God!"

Thomas Caldecot Chubb

139.

Un marcennaio intende a grandeggiare

When a low lout decides to be upstart
And puffs his chest and swells vaingloriously,
Folk can't abide him acting this new part;
They can't abide his strutting vanity.
"Make him go back," they say, "to his old art
Of beating wool out as in days gone by;
If he don't make our heads ache devilishly,
He stirs up rumblings in our hinderpart."
Think then if I do wrong when I complain
At the foul stink — a most foul stink, it was —
I suffer from this lewd wretch Lapo Pagno.
To see him preen and play the gentleman
Makes me all hot to flee as far as Bagno,
And that's nigh distant as the Abruzzi is.

140.

De guata ben, Ciampol, questa vecchiuzza

Ugh, do observe that ancient hag, Ciampól.
No other half so foul you're like to meet.
Yet see her strut and swell. Upon my soul
She cannot know her odor is not sweet.
I' faith, she seems a very Barbary ape,
And is one too, in gestures, form, and face.
Just look at her. She'll twist as at some jape
Her ugly mug into a lewd grimace.
Therefore, you should not tear your heart out so
With anger, or, with anguish, or with love
That for rejoicing you do not have room.
Why? Just this marvel which will end your gloom!
Seeing her does, and has, and will remove
All amorous thoughts, and this you ought to know.

141.

Salute manda lo tu' Buon Martini

For Buon Martini, you I thus salute,
Berto Renier, from stinking Germany:
Please know that fine Greek wine's no more for me;
Instead I drink foul beer of ill repute.
I've changed great rooms and gardens rich with fruit
For frost and plaguing flies and winter mud.
I wear rough cloth a country bumpkin would
Who once was linen-clad from head to foot.
Yes, you can scorn my shabby life indeed
Since we do not even one napkin have
When seven of us dine from the same plate,
And as we have no cloak to serve this need,
We dry our hands on sleeve after we lave
And so remain grease-stained from head to pate.

142.

Le gioi' ch'i t'ho recate da Veneza

The jewels I've brought from Venice, take you, if,
Ghinuccia, you're not with me always now.
Meo, you know that we have had a tiff
So you can no more say you're mine, you know!
Alas, love, for you fragrant are as spice.
It's like a boil to have you say you'll shake me.
Even if you should make me queen of Greece,
I'll not be as I once was. Try to take me!
None the less, I'll not leave your doorstep ever
Unless you tell me why. Instead I'll kill me,
And you will then be asked: "Who caused befall this?"
My mother beat me nor did you endeavor
To save me. So go hang yourself. 'T would thrill me
And always will as long as I recall this.

Thomas Caldecot Chubb

143.

Pelle chiabelle di Dio, no ci arvai

"By the Cross' nails, don't set your stumps down there
Now that you've carvified that lad from Rome!"
"Lucca's my home address. What's the good word here?"
"Squash? Who wants squash? I'm sent to peddle some."
"Woolhead, come tell us how you go and where?"
"To Arezzo, dolt, to peddle this apple for gain."
"I bought this she-ass from a barrel maker,
A Pistolese, and now I'll clip her mane."
"The evil eye on you, you harlot's brat,
Of which in Florence you can buy a peck
For one *denaio* with a melon thrown in."
"By Christ, my beast is laden, he'll break his back,
But I'll still to Siena, and that's that,
To sell my fruit before decay sets in."

144.

Ogni capretto ritorn'a su' latte

Does not each kid return to mother's teat
Though he may wander for a little while?
If father, then, and son each other assail,
If brother thrusts at brother in white heat,
If nephew and uncle, housetop tomcats, claw,
If wives their husbands, husbands their wives beat,
If cousins cry to cousins: "I'll go to law!"
Soon they make peace and all is calm and sweet.
Therefore I counsel you for your own good
'Twixt this and that one never intervene
Though each with sword the other seeks to hack.
There is no tighter bond to bind than blood,
And when their anger's gone, all is serene.
To mother's teat, I say, each kid comes back.

145.

A cosa fatta non vale pentère

It's waste of time a past deed to repent,
Nor can one say: "Here's what I should have done!"
Hindsight's not worth a thing to anyone.
A man must be forewarned before the event.
The one who's started on the downward way
Can never climb again to his old niche.
I, then, lost soul and surely gone astray,
In that place where naught itches me, must scratch.
For I have fallen and can never rise,
Nor have I either friend or relative
Who'll reach a hand out to lift up my head,
Yet I still say — think it not jesting-wise —
"Would that my lady more love to me would give
Than I, in any sonnet, ever said."

146.

Egli è sì poco di fede e d'amore

There is so little charity today
Or faith still in the hearts of poor mankind
That: "There is none!" one could quite truthfully say
And thus describe all you could readily find.
If you do ill, men call you good and great,
Nor could you find a brother or a friend
Who even a single copper coin would spend
To make you emperor, or soon or late.
You don't believe me? Well, then, try this out.
Go to the very dearest comrade you have,
And then come back tell me he gave you his pelf.
"I thought that he was generous, the lout,
The miser, the pinchpenny!" I hear you rave.
"He's generous indeed — but to himself."

Thomas Caldecot Chubb

147.

Senno non val a cui fortuna è cònta

Sense is not needed if fortune smile on you,
And if you are ill-starred it is worth naught,
But sense is not bestowed upon one who
Does not please fortune, by her is not sought.
For fortune is the one who up and down
Goes, and who gives and straightway takes away.
She shames one, to another brings a crown.
She can make even a fool seem wise, they say.
And often times have I seen it transpire
That one who uses sense is deemed wittold
While he who uses none takes off the prize.
If fortune, then, deems that you should go higher.
You cannot fail. This must be, it is told.
To wait upon her pleasure then is wise.

148.

Stando lo baldovino dentro un prato

A jackass in a meadow one bright morn
Was feasting on the fresh and tender grass
When he looked down, and lo, as in a glass,
He saw his image, but each ear seemed a horn.
"I am Sir Stag," he said, and all upborne
With pride, cried also: "Watch me leap this ditch!"
He gave a bound to do it, instead of which
He landed in the middle, damp, and forlorn.
Oh what a loud bray he emitted then!
"Alas! Alas! Ah woe is me! Ah woe!
I really am a donkey, a big fool!"
So dolts are who pretend to be wise men,
But make them show you what they think they know.
You'll see them as they are. They still need school.

Chi de l'altrui farina fa lasagne

Who makes his pasta from another's grain
Is like a castle without wall or moat.
His wits are as befogged to me 't is plain
As one who buys a walnut for chestnut.
Nor are his words less frail than spider-web
Who insults, saying: "None will insult me!"
He has no teeth, and wants to gnaw ox rib,
Or make high peak from plains that level be.
But, God knows, such thoughts have not ever soiled,
The one who has no courage in his heart.
He knows that reckless souls find only ill
And rather does as one, who, battle embroiled,
Hides behind shield till foe's lance shivers apart,
Then shows how great in combat is his skill.

I. Simone da Siena to Cecco

Cecco, se Deo t'allegri di Becchina

Cecco, if God should give you a good hour
With your Becchina, and other good news, too,
Tell me about it who feel pain anew
And have a heart that's ground like coarsest flour.
For if I do not soon have medicine,
I greatly fear that from my ills, I'll die —
I who am wrapped in so much melancholy
That I slide downward where there's no incline.
Nor can I ever from the straight way go
That all do not cry out: "A madman, he!"
'T is Love that me down this dire path has sent.
In God's name tell me then, who've walked it too
And walk it still if you speak truth to me,
What guard has any if Love does not relent?

Thomas Caldecot Chubb

II. Cecco's reply

Questo ti manda a dir Cecco, Simone

This is what Cecco answers you, Simón,
Since you would know just what his guard has been:
He's suffered patiently, without, within,
Each blow Love's dealt him many a long season.
For out of his own mouth said Solomon
These words which you must understand and know:
"The full felt weight of evil is only known
As much as into your heart you let it go."
Therefore, if to Siena you ever return,
Be you not broken, but to the blows bend
If grief comes on you yet another time.
The prize in love or in aught else to earn,
'Another life must be the master of you'
As Cato tells us in his doggerel rhyme.

APPENDIX

Persons and Places*

5 Becchina. Daughter of the leather tanner Benci, and the lady of Cecco's sonnets.

9 Moco. Probably Moco di Pietro Tolomei. The Tolomei were one of Siena's important families.

9 Ciampolin. Ciampolino (John Paul). Unidentified Sienese who was first Cecco's friend, then his bitter enemy.

9 Mino di Pepo Accoridori. A member of the Petroni family. Cardinal Petroni supposedly protected Cecco during his exile.

9 Tan'. Tano, a Sienese known for his pugnacity. The reference is ironic as he was greatly feared.

9 Migo. Not identified, but also a Sienese.

19 Michael. The archangel Michael.

24 Benci. Becchina's father.

24. Mita, Torella, Nello, Poggese. Unidentified, but the first two were probably women, and Nello is a Sienese name.

31 Messina. In Sicily. There was a well-known lighthouse there to guide ships through the turbulent strait.

34 Colle. A town between Siena and Florence. The Sienese hated it because on June 8, 1269 they suffered a terrible defeat there.

39 Christ's kerchief. The Veronica or handkerchief on which the Lord wiped his face on the way to Calvary. This left the imprint of his face.

40 Brother Angiolier'. Cecco's father Angioliero.

*The number in the left hand column is that of the sonnet in which the name first appeared.

Thomas Caldecot Chubb

45 Archidos'. Archidossi, an important castle in Sienese territory.

45 Montegiuovi. The same.

46 Fucecchio. A small town near Empoli in the Arno valley. Mountains completely cut it off from any possible sight of Bologna.

46 Pugna. A village in the Arbia valley near Siena.

46 Boccheggian'. Boccheggiano, a very small mining town hidden deeply in the mountains southeast of Siena.

53 St. John. St. John the Divine, not St. John the Baptist.

97 Geatto. A noted highwayman of the day.

101 Taddeo. Taddeo Alderotti, a famous Florentine doctor who founded the Bologna school of medicine. Although he may be the Taddeo placed in heaven in *Paradiso* XII,83, Dante speaks scornfully of his translation of Aristotle's *Ethics* in *Convivio* I,x,10.

102 Mino Piero. Giacomino Pieri dei Colombini. His grandson founded the Order of Gesuati, known as the Aquavitae Brothers because of the liquor they distilled.

102 Galen and Hippocrates. The latter was the supposed founder of medicine, the former a famous Greek physician.

102 Donato. Aelius Donatus, a Roman scholar and grammarian of the fourth century.

105 Fra Paglaio. A popular Sienese preacher of the Pagliaresi family.

108 That other Cecco. Fortarrigo. Cecco Fortarrigo, the Boccaccio scapegrace Cecco. See *Decamerone* IX,4. Fortarrigo is his father.

108 Enoch and Elijah. The prophets who were carried up to heaven (to live there eternally) while they were still alive.

112 Lucca's Holy Face. An ancient picture of Christ, one supposedly done in his lifetime, which was greatly venerated in Lucca.

114 Chiana. The river in the valley from which Chianti comes. Its eels were supposed to be indigestible.

118 Lan'. Arcolano di Squarcia di Ridolfi Maconi whom Dante puts in the hell of the spendthrifts in *Inferno* XIII,120.

122 Corso from Corzano. Corzano is a little village near Siena. Corso cannot be identified.

125 Piero, Giovanni and Martino. The modern equivlent would be Tom, Dick, and Harry.

126 Tese. Cortese dei Tolomei. An enemy of Ciampolino.

126 San Pellegrino. There are several places in Tuscany known by this name.

128 Capoccio. The counterfeiter mentioned by Dante in *Inferno* XXIX,133.

128 Branca. Not identified. Certainly not Dante's Brancca. He lived in Genoa.

129 Pina. One of Mino Zeppa's lady loves.

131 Pier Fasteo. Said to be an ancestor of the Bandinelli family, he supposedly had, like Messer Torello of Istria in *Decamerone* X,9, the power of being transported by magic from the Near East to Italy in a night, thus anticipating Alitalea.

131 Lodi and Pavia. North Italian towns.

132 Radi cowards. Cecco plays with their real name, Placidi, to assume that they were poltroons, and Mino Zeppa one of them.

134 Nicolo Pescé. According to Sicilian legend, Cola Pescé (Nick Fish) became half fish and found wondrous things when he swam under the island of Sicily.

Thomas Caldecot Chubb

135 The puffed-up Captain. Diego de la Rat who terrorized Florence after the White Guelphs had been driven out and Dante exiled.

135 King Charles, the lord Count of Provence. Probably Charles II of Naples.

138 Nero Picciolin'. Neri Picciolini, a Sienese merchant of modest means. Not one of the magnates.

139 Lapo Pagno. A lowborn peasant who pretended he was a gentleman.

139 Bagno. The baths of Pozzuoli near Naples. You had made it if you could afford to go there.

139 Abruzzi. A mountainous region which forms the spine of Italy.

141 Buon Martini. Nothing is known of him.

141 Berto Renier. Thought to be one of the Ricasoli, and distantly related to Cecco.

142 Ghinuccia and Meo. Cecco had a son named Meo. If this is he, he was as scapegrace as his father. Ghinuccia, not otherwise identified, could have been one of his ladies.

150 Simone di Siena. Nothing is known of him.

150 Cato. Not the Roman Cato, but the author of the *Disticha Catonio,* one Dionysius Cato who in the fifth century wrote a rhymed text book for school children. It was still used in Cecco's time.